The Moral Case against Religious Belief

The Moral Case against Religious Belief

R.A.Sharpe

SCM PRESS LTD

0 334 02680 6

First published 1997 by
SCM Press Ltd
9–17 St Albans Place London N1 0NX

Typeset at The Spartan Press Ltd,
Lymington, Hants
Printed in Great Britain by
Biddles Ltd, Guildford and King's Lynn

For Lynne

Contents

Preface

'Nothing to kill or die for – and no religion too'

(John Lennon, 'Imagine')

In most long books there is a short book trying to get out. I tried to liberate the short book by resisting, rather easily, the temptation to write a long scholarly work with an equally long reading list attached. This is a book for what publishers call the 'general public' and it is intended to be of a length that can be read in an evening or even at a sitting, though I hope that it invites reflections which will go on rather longer. What I have to say is largely directed at the Christian faith, though it may apply to Judaism or Islam as well. I do not know enough about these other faiths to say. I write as a post-Christian.

I have avoided much in the way of references, footnotes and the business of a bibliography. This is partly because this is not intended as a scholarly work but it is also because religion and its philosophy is not an area on which I am qualified to write *qua* scholar. But, as you will soon be aware, religion has been of intense importance to me all my life. I have been immersed in it, and nearly forty years of atheism have not eradicated the deep effect it had on me. My relationship to it is very ambivalent.

Of my debts, apart from the well meaning people with whom I spent my childhood, I owe a good deal to my colleagues at a neighbouring campus of the University of Wales, to Dick Beardsmore and Professor D.Z.Phillips of Swansea (though, should D.Z. come to read this, he will disapprove of it), to Professor Colin Radford of the University of Kent who, as a sixth-former in the same rural grammar school, inserted the knife which gradually cut the bonds which separated me from my Christian faith, and finally to my wife, Lynne, who is a militant atheist in a way I am not and who has never been willing to acknowledge that there is more to religion than a collection of fairy-tales. But she and I have discussed these matters interminably and she has had an important influence on what I say.

I

Religion and Morality

I

Sometimes I am asked, usually by Christian believers, whether I believe in God. When I give, amongst my reasons for not believing in God, moral reasons, people are apt to be surprised. Of course, the very idea that one has reasons for believing in God is somewhat odd. I don't think anybody is nowadays persuaded to believe in God by a catalogue of reasons comparable, say, to the reasons I might give to show why capital punishment is wrong or why it is a mistake to suppose that large inequalities of income in a society are for the general benefit of the poor, as well as more obviously for the rich. Perhaps once reasons persuaded people into theism, but even that seems to me somewhat doubtful. Rather, I think that those people who believe in God believe because they find it hard not to believe and people like myself are atheists because they find it impossible to believe. We do not choose to believe, nor do we choose not to believe.

So what is the point of my arguments in this book? Well, I hope to persuade those whose faith is somewhat frail and those who, though believers, have some independence of mind; I claim that religious belief does not necessarily make its possessor an authority on matters moral and that spokesmen and spokeswomen for religion are often badly wrong about moral questions as a result of their religious commitment. But more strongly still, I shall be arguing that in some ways morality is corrupted by religion.

I said that people are surprised when I say that I am a 'moral atheist' (not in the sense that I am a moral man and an atheist but rather in the sense that my particular form of atheism is a moral atheism). I am not very surprised that they are surprised and, as a beginning, I shall discuss some of the reasons for their astonishment.

The first reason is that in our culture religion and morality are very closely intertwined. There is a very deep presumption in our culture that Christianity got morality right. Some testimony to this is to be found in the fact that those Victorians who rebelled against the metaphysical claims of religion nevertheless continued to hold on to Christian morality. They might have denied the existence of God, the special place of man in the natural world, the possibility of immortality, the truth of the account of the Passion and Resurrection, but they still thought that the Beatitudes gave us as good a pattern for life as we can find. To be merciful, to be a peacemaker, to love your enemies, to give your alms in secret and not to judge others seemed to them, as it does to many including myself, the mark of a good man or a good woman.

Moreover the Christian God is a moral God. In some religions, particularly polytheistic religions, the gods are not necessarily paragons of virtue. Jupiter behaved much like a very powerful tyrant who was also able to turn himself into a bull or whatever in order to get his own way. He was under the sway of anger or lust as we are. But in a culture based upon Christianity, Judaism or Islam, God is assumed to be both just and above reproach and also to have a very intimate concern with the behaviour of human beings. He is very much concerned as to whether or not they sin. So beliefs in God and moral standards go together. Therefore to suggest that I might have moral reasons for not believing in God is apt to sound peculiar. It suggests that I do not think that our conception of God is a conception of a Being who is just, and this, you will rightly think, is an impossibility. This I do not dispute. My moral qualms about religion are different.

The assumed connection between religion and morality comes out in all sorts of ways in our society. Any debate on questions of morality is thought to require a rabbi, a minister or a priest as a spokesman. There is an assumption that in virtue of their place in a religious organization, these people are qualified to pronounce on questions of morality. They may or may not regard themselves as experts. In the Roman Catholic Church there are people who are regarded as experts and are called upon to advise on moral dilemmas, but this is not to be found in all sects. Furthermore, religion has a privileged position in other ways; certain practices, such as male infant circumcision without anaesthetic, or, possibly, halal butchery, are not forbidden by law but permitted solely because they are enshrined in religious ritual. Otherwise they certainly would be, because they are cruel.

Indeed even amongst atheists, it is widely assumed that morality and religion go together. This comes out very forcibly in a topic I intend to discuss later on this book, sexual morality. We all know that the official position of the Roman Catholic Church is that artificial birth control is

3

morally wrong. Obviously most people in Britain, including most Roman Catholics, dissent. They think that the idea that it is sinful to use a condom is absurd. But what they will not conclude is what I think they ought to conclude, and that is that the papal embargo on contraception itself is morally wrong. They think it remains a moral option. They might even regard not using artificial contraception as morally praiseworthy in a way which goes beyond the ordinary requirements for moral behaviour. It is like the papal view of virginity. Virginity is not required, but it does reflect well on the individual concerned. It is a 'higher calling'. To use the technical term of philosophers, it is a matter of 'supererogation'. The acts of a hero or a saint are supererogatory; they go beyond what can ordinarily be regarded as a duty. Eschewing contraception won't count as highly as sacrificing one's life to save a child, of course, but it probably is rather better than giving up smoking for Lent and a lot better than merely not taking the largest slice of fruit cake at tea. (I hasten to add that I am describing what I gauge to be the views of ordinary Catholics; they are not the views of the Pope, as far as I can see.)

So we are predisposed to think of religion and morality as intimately connected and reluctant to condemn as immoral even moral views which are confused, inconsistent and which cause human suffering, as does the papal teaching on contraception. (The arguments against the ban on contraception are obvious enough; I will content myself with pointing out that if what is wicked is frustrating the proper purpose of intercourse [which is procreation], then that purpose is equally frustrated by the rhythm method.)

The second quite basic assumption many people in our culture make is that religious commitment brings about higher moral standards. A friend of mine who is both a philosopher and a Christian gave a lecture at my university defending the view that Christians are more trustworthy than atheists. Yet those who adhere to this idea will not deny that amongst religious people we can find the very good, the very bad and the merely indifferent. The crimes committed by deeply religious people are innumerable and often peculiarly horrible. As I write sectarian divisions blight Ulster. There we have the extraordinary spectacle of Protestants emerging from a church service to throw stones at those police who seek to prevent them from marching through a Catholic area, a march intended to assert their dominance. They walk out of a church whose founder told them to love their enemies and turn the other cheek intent on abusing and humiliating neighbours who belong to another branch of the same religion. And yet hardly a week goes by without somebody declaiming that the loss of religion is responsible for the growth of crime, divorce and immorality in our society. They think that if more people believed in God and practised religion there would be less theft, less violence and less divorce.

Now I suspect that the relationship between religion and crime is very complicated indeed. For years a higher proportion of crime in the United Kingdom was committed by those of Irish descent and who were almost invariably Roman Catholics. No doubt there are social reasons for this. Understandably Irish people have a long tradition of regarding the law as an alien imposition and no doubt the police expected to find criminals amongst the Irish community. On the other side, I would be very surprised if a Strict Baptist or a Pentecostalist or a Plymouth Brother (sects amongst which I was brought up) was to be found guilty of theft, because I know enough about the pressure to be a witness to God's saving power amongst these communities. This is not to say it cannot happen, but I do think it must be rarer than it would be amongst Christians who belong to less demanding branches of the church. The church which expects high standards is likely to get them. So I certainly would expect that converts to some branches of religious organizations will show a marked improvement in meeting certain rules. No theft, backbiting, swearing or lying for a start. What it may not produce is the more complex moral behaviour which shows an imaginative understanding of different patterns of life. But of that more anon.

So I do not deny that many religious people are morally good people nor will I deny that much good has been done in the world by people who would not have done what they have done if they had not been motivated by religion. Still, I can allow the last point without saying that they necessarily acted morally in bringing about good.

This will sound paradoxical but consider. A beggar is lying in the street with undressed sores. (Make it a London street, since the moral advances of the past decade and a half make it as likely there as in Calcutta.) Three people come along. The first is motivated to dress his wounds because she is moved by his needs and his suffering. The second is disgusted and repelled but, nevertheless, pulls herself together and remembers the moral injunction that we should care for those who are less well off than ourselves and finds some ointment and bandages. The third asks himself 'What does Jesus want me to do?' In a parallel situation he would have helped the beggar. So the passer-by does.

Which of these acts morally? We might say that all three do because, all things being equal, all of them do some good. But I have qualms about the last. My qualms are precisely because his reaction is mediated by a theological consideration. The first case is, in my view, unambiguously moral. She sees a need and she responds. The second case is a bit more problematic. We might imagine that the second passer-by recognizes a lack of sympathy in her make-up and is determined to try to do something about it and, to that extent, we admire her. But the third Samaritan acts because he has an overarching belief system which tells him how to act in this way. He might not think it through in quite the terms I have described. There are other ways in which his religious commitment might motivate him. But my example requires that he be motivated to act the way he does by his faith. As George Herbert's hymn says:

'Who sweeps a room, as for thy laws
Makes that and the action fine.'

When I said that, I do not deny the obvious, that many, possibly most, Christians are good people. For one thing, even if they have beliefs like the third Samaritan, those may not be the beliefs which make them act when they come across somebody in need. On such occasions they act out of compassion and they act morally. In such a case their Christian beliefs will be at best what Wittgenstein called an idly spinning wheel; they play no part in the motivation. At worst they interfere.

Now sometimes the results of the interference may be horrendous. We are all sometimes in the position of having to hurt somebody or some animal in a way which goes against whatever compassion there is in our nature. You may have to hurt a cat or a dog in treating a wound. When in such cases we set aside our own reluctance to cause pain in terms of the greater good we do what, presumably, the inaptly named Pope Innocent might have been doing when he permitted the Catholic Church to use torture. The pain caused was supposed to be in the greater good. I don't suppose there are many people who nowadays think that morally right, though perhaps some members of Opus Dei do.

What I cannot understand is how it cannot be obvious and certain that to torture a man is wicked. I cannot understand how somebody could be less certain about this than he is about the truths of a religious doctrine. How can somebody be more convinced that heretics ought to be burned than he is that torturing people in such a way is wicked? One fact about religious commitment and conflict is, of course, that it leads its adherents to set aside such ordinary reactions as compassion for the suffering. What otherwise leads the Serbian Orthodox to murder Muslim Bosnians or Protestant Ulstermen to murder Catholic Ulstermen? To suppose that we can be as certain of theological claims as we are of the wrongness of torturing somebody with whom we disagree is already to have been corrupted by those theological dogmas.

Finally, I have heard it argued on behalf of religion that, no matter how bad a man may be, without his religion he would be worse. Nancy Mitford wrote in her letter to Pamela Berry on 17 May 1950:

So I had Evelyn (Waugh) from Friday morning to Monday and still love him though at one point I felt obliged to ask how he reconciles being so horrible with being a Christian. He replied rather sadly that were he not a Christian he would be even more horrible (difficult) . . .

The problem is that we do not know how this could be shown. In the case of many religious men (particularly converts like Waugh and Muggeridge) it is, as Nancy Mitford says, difficult to see that they would be worse without their religion and, in the case of many converts, religion seems to have had a deleterious effect on their behaviour. Religion, as we can see, gives them something more to be obnoxious about. In fact some of the great 'saints' of the church, men like St Bernard, are people most of us would go a very long way to avoid (in the latter case not least because a smell of stale vomit always clung about his person). All that I can say is that amongst those of my acquaintances who I think of as unquestionably and uncomplicatedly good I include atheists more often than religious men or women.

There remain, of course, a small class of people whom, whilst I do not share their beliefs, I can only admire. Who is not moved by the courage of Bonhoeffer? I once heard Bishop Wilson of Birmingham being interviewed on the radio. He was asked how he managed to forgive those who ill-treated him when he was a prisoner in a Japanese concentration camp. He replied that they were once children and he tried to think of them as they once were, adding that nobody can hate a child. Although I am uncertain about the viability of this kind of reasoning, here was a man determined to live by the Christian doctrine of forgiveness and finding a way by which he could put it into action. That one remark is worth the entire corpus of St Ignatius of

Loyola's *Spiritual Exercises* or Thomas à Kempis's *Imitation of Christ*.

II

This is not a treatise on ethics, but something needs to be said about how I conceive of morality. Needless to say, books have been written about it. This is not the place for a lengthy discussion, but since Christian ethics tends to make certain dubious assumptions, some debate cannot be avoided. I think of morality widely. It is connected both with what we should or should not do and with what it is to flourish or live well. Both these aspects of morality will enter into the subsequent discussion. Although I shall suggest that some of the injunctions of the churches are objectionable, on the whole I do not dissent from the pattern of moral life set down in the Beatitudes. My objection is much more that to live a moral life in a theological context is not to live the best sort of life.

There is a tendency for Christians to think of morality in terms of a set of rules. Obviously the Ten Commandments are rules. In an intensely Non-Conformist home, my life as a child was largely encompassed by rules. There were things which we could do and things which we could not do on a Sunday. I could not go out to play, could not listen to jazz or opera but could listen to other classical music. My mother could write family letters and post them but not read the Sunday newspaper and so on. I have no doubt that this was viewed as a moral matter.

Equally important, though not more important, was the embargo on lying. Telling the truth was required at all times. But an exceptionless rule against lying means, for example, that you cannot tell an untruth to save another man's life or, more trivially, avoid a pointless insult to somebody whose garden you are invited to admire. The problems are very familiar. It is easy to think up exceptions to most moral rules. If indeed you try to maintain an absolute injunction against lying you end with something worse, something like the corruption of your moral judgment.

Here is an eminent Roman Catholic thinker, P.T.Geach, on the topic:

> If we read the lives of the Saints, we see how they managed to avoid lying in crises. St Athanasius was rowing on a river when the persecutors came rowing in the opposite direction. 'Where is the traitor Athanasius?' 'Not far away,' the Saint gaily replied and rowed past them undetected.

What Geach is advocating here is economy with the truth. His saint deceived his enemies. Of course, I think the saint was right to do so. But to pretend that his deception does not have the same purpose and effect as an open lie is to allow your concern for the letter to obscure your judgment of the substantial moral issue. In doing that one's judgment is corrupted.

Secondly, if you think of morality as Christians generally do, as a set of injunctions which are laid upon us by the Bible, the church or the Pope, you find yourself in other difficulties. A rule is either observed or broken. So any action which falls under it is right or wrong. The Roman Catholic rules on divorce, abortion and contraception do not allow of borderline cases. A frozen foetus consisting of eight cells, which is certainly living tissue once it has been defrosted but hardly what we would normally call a human being, counts as an unborn child which it is murder to kill. There are no borderline cases here. Yet Christians might profitably read the record of Jesus's attitude to the rules and regulations of orthodoxy which seem, by comparison, very relaxed.

There is a much more important point which bears more deeply on what will follow. It is best introduced by an example. Imagine a woman married to a man who is sporadically and unpredictably violent. Should she leave him or put up with it? You can alter the example as you choose so as to make it plausible. Maybe her life or health is in danger, maybe not. Maybe he is psychologically dependent upon her, maybe not. Maybe he shows affection and remorse after, maybe not. We can imagine that the woman consults her family and friends and perhaps a priest, a psychiatrist or a doctor. But in the end we may feel that rules will not cater for this case. There are just so many contingencies that no rules will be formulated in advance which will say whether or not she should leave him. Now, perhaps you are not convinced. Perhaps you think that a rule could be formulated which would meet our moral intuitions about this and, indeed, somebody in the Vatican might now be engaged on doing this.

Now whether or not a rule can be formulated is neither here nor there in the end. Because whatever advice the woman takes, the decision in the end will be hers and hers alone. Such moral decisions become hard and lonely just when the decision is the responsibility of the individual. Now I am inclined to say that she has to work through the issue herself, considering as clearly as she can all the reasons for and against. She must not pay either too much or too little regard to her own interests. If you like, there are rules of method but not rules for conduct. If she does all this she will come out with the right answer. (I am not going to say that it is 'the right answer for her' because it might not be – it might be against her interests.) Somebody else might, in the same situation, come out with a different answer. But we would still be inclined to say that it is the right answer. They might weight factors differently. One woman might be inclined to put up with the fear and misery for the sake of a commitment, the other not; and who are we to say, from the outside, that one is right and the other wrong? The important point is that the rightness of the decision is guaranteed by the way in which it is reached. Philosophers would say that the rightness or wrongness of the decision is internally related to the method by which it is obtained.

Not all, perhaps not even many, moral decisions are like this, of course. Perhaps fortunately we spend most of our lives making decisions which are reasonably straightforward. But some decisions are hard, and hard decisions are often like this. The decision to break off a relationship before marriage, the decision to have an abortion, changing one's career, leaving a political party or leaving a church for another one should all involve this sort of appraisal. Whatever the woman does she might feel remorse. I would not say that the remorse is rational or irrational. It might be either. Sometimes remorse is just something one has to live with. It will get less acute as time passes. I suspect that it is a quite common experience that when somebody you love constantly hurts you, your love for him gradually diminishes. Eventually, even if you believe in the permanence of the relationship and want to go on loving him, you find that you do not. It is as though scar tissue grows over the wound.

We have been thinking of what we should or should not do. These are matters of judgment and action. But religion also prescribes for us an ideal of a good life. To live well is, *inter alia*, to live morally, and on this atheists and religious people need not disagree. The man who is cruel and capricious, no matter how successful in worldly terms, does not live a good life. As it is sometimes put, he does not flourish. This is why the old question 'Why should I act morally?' can only be raised seriously by those who fail to understand what it is to live well. The good life is a moral life, and any other is a life which is not worth living. To live a good life also requires love. To flourish demands above all that love should have a central place in my life, that I should care for others and have passions and interests which are not self-centred. Sigmund Freud was once asked how, given the human heritage of neuroses and conflicts, a man could live a decent life. He replied, with rather uncharacteristic wisdom, 'love and work'. Freud was right. These are preconditions for a good life. Happiness or contentment, of course, is something else. I may suffer from illness or from the illness and premature death of those whom I love. My work may not flourish. Happiness may not be a prize I attain. But, happy or not, a good life is not led by those who seek power for its own sake or the accumulation of wealth without consideration for others.

Some of us, through no fault of our own, find a good life harder to lead than others. The matter of character comes in here. For some of us kindness is not something we strive for. We are naturally kind and, perhaps, naturally forgiving. The nastiness of others does not rankle. It is not because we don't allow it to that it does not play on our minds. It just does not. But other people have to fight feelings of resentment all their lives. Niceness is not natural to them. Such a person may be good through gritted teeth. Niceness is one natural advantage that some of us enjoy. There are others. I myself have little doubt that physical prowess, intelligence and good looks are advantages, though those who have them may be 'spoilt', as we would say. But these are to some extent unlike niceness; though there is little we can do to develop good looks or intelligence, we can get ourselves out of thinking ill of others – though it may take some effort.

So religion offers a vision of the good life, though in some respects it is a vision disputed by non-believers. David Hume did not have much time for what he called 'monkish virtues' such as celibacy, self-denial and humility. Nor do I. But I have a wider brief in this book. I am not going to claim that religious believers are precluded from living a good life; but I do think that their profession places obstacles in their path and the obstacles are the greater the more intense their beliefs. Bunyan's Pilgrim lost his burden at the cross; but the cross also imposes a burden on believers. The more intense a believer's commitment, the harder it is for him to commit some offences, but the easier it is for him to commit others. Obviously intolerance and the persecution of others are examples. To the extent that your beliefs are held with great fervour, the fact that others disagree or even find you irrational is an offence. The way a believer explains this away is by saying that those who disagree with him are blinded by pride, or self-deception, or even by Satan. Thus Roman Catholics are apt to say to me that if I were to look at the claims of their church without prejudice I would be convinced of the truth of their beliefs. (Which I deny, of course.) But perhaps less obvious is that the religious life demands time spent in spiritual exercises such as prayer, Bible-reading, going to services and, worst of all, in proselytizing. These are burdens. When I was a Christian I found them mostly boring and, as far as the last was concerned, positively painful. Others might feel differently, I suppose. But however they feel about it, these variants of what Hume might have called monkish virtues impose burdens which leads me to have misgivings as to whether the resulting life is a good one.

The final problem which you may find in the idea that my reasons for not believing are moral is perhaps the most obvious, and those of you who have been following the argument have probably been waiting impatiently for me to address it. It goes like this. Whether or not God exists is some sort of fact independent of us. But what I judge to be good or bad behaviour and what I judge to be the good life is a matter of value. Surely questions of value and questions of existence are independent. David Hume famously remarked on the fallacy of moving from what is the case to what ought to be the case. Am I not committing the converse fallacy, of moving from what ought to be the case to what is the case? For on the basis of moral objections both to what religion regards as the good life and to some of the particular injunctions laid on us by the Christian church, I set myself up as an atheist. Surely this must be a *non-sequitur*. The assumed independence of the two questions of moral value and existence is reflected in some of the most famous remarks in the history of philosophical reflection on God. The atheist Holbach, asked what he would say if, contrary to his supposition, he found himself in the presence of God, replied that he would say to God, 'How dare you?' ('How dare you create a world with such suffering.') John Stuart Mill observed:

> I will call no being good who is not what I mean when I apply that epithet to my fellow-creatures; and if such a being can sentence me to hell for not so calling him, to hell will I go.

Both writers keep the question of moral values and of God's existence separate.

But look at the way we actually talk of God. If I were to say to the average churchgoer that God has instructed me to assemble an arsenal in order that I, with some followers, should set about killing unbelievers, he would reply in horror and amazement, 'But God could not have commanded you to do that.' Notice the 'could not'. This is not a matter of fact to be decided by some appeal to observation, a text or an authority. On his conception God *cannot* be like that.

My point is that we settle many questions about the character of God by deciding what moral qualities are to be admired and concluding that God must have them. The sub-text is that only a being who had these qualities could properly be worshipped. So God must enshrine our moral values. In this way we make him in our own ideal image. We cannot extricate the question of the nature of God from an inquiry into what are our moral values. The two are not independent. (Some believers worship God from fear, of course, but I take it that this is not typical of mature religions in which 'perfect love casteth out fear'; rather, fear is associated with superstition.) If I value intellectual honesty, then that must also be enshrined in my concept of God. 'Tell me what your God is like and I will tell you who you are.'

So the riposte which many readers probably anticipated, that by offering moral arguments against religion I have not offered a reason for not believing in God, is not an argument which will wash. His existence is not a matter separate from how we should act and what we should value. The separate question is whether a powerful agent created the world. But that is a question of fact which may or may not be settled; if it can be settled, it will be settled as scientific questions are settled. And if we decided in the affirmative, nothing would follow about our duty to worship that agent. We would have no more reason to worship him (or her or it) than we have to worship the spiral nebula in Andromeda.

So we are now equipped with the minimum required to set out on a consideration of the ethics of religious belief. But before we do so, I had better warn the reader that the debate will be a collection of rather disparate considerations. There is no tight and tidy construction to this argument. In some ways Christian morality is admirable and in some respects not. I have two main charges to make. First of all, I believe that what religion requires of us in the name of morality, when pursued in detail, does not make sense. For the Christian virtues frequently involve dragging moral ideas out of their normal context into a setting in which they lose the connections that give them meaning for us. Any philosopher will recognize in this the influence of Wittgenstein. But Wittgenstein was generally more charitable to religion than I am inclined to be.

I shall argue, then, that when we are told that the good life involves loving God, we use the idea of love in a new context where it ceases to have the sense it usually has. The initial reaction of the believer may well be that when she talks about loving God she knows what she means; she knows what her religious experience is and what she says, even if obscure, will not be meaningless. But things are not quite that easy. The problem is that we are tempted to think that what we say has a meaning which is given by what we intend to say. The man in the street, when finding it hard to express something, thinks of it in just those terms. He has a thought; the thought may be quite clear in itself but he lacks either the resources or the skill to get it across. Perhaps the language itself is at fault; it just does not have the vocabulary he needs. Words fail him. So, the idea continues, when we talk of God and of the Christian experience of God or of God's forgiveness, naturally we are foiled time and time again by the limitations of our language. It then becomes a matter of shipping in words like 'father', 'shepherd' and 'love', amongst many others, which become slightly adjusted in their new context. It is not the case that there is nothing to be sensibly communicated; the fault lies not in us but in our language.

But what we want to say and the words we use to say it are not at all unconnected. What would it be, as Wittgenstein once observed, to use the word 'cold' and mean by it 'warm'? I am not, of course, suggesting for a moment that there is a prison-house of language which walls us in and from which we cannot escape. We can and do invent new words where a need exists. But such capacities are limited precisely because the thoughts we have we have because we have a language first. When we take a word like 'just' or 'love' or 'know-ledge' out of its framework in our ordinary business of life and apply it to a being who does not share the life we live, does not share our physical and mental limitations, our social setting and our biological nature, we cannot guarantee a sense of the words we use. They will crack and bend under the powerful forces of a new setting. It is the task of the philosopher to make this plain. We may think we are using them meaningfully, but we are deceived, and it is philosophical questioning which will show to us how we are mistaken.

Of course, it is a mistake to think that a sentence either makes sense or is nonsense. It is not quite that simple. It is not an all-or-nothing affair. I recently reviewed a book in which sentences like the following appear:

> When music and musicians accomplish their real function, the result is a *hierophany*. The work, the performers and the listeners disappear, all submerged in an eternal present, in the flow of cosmic affectivity which emanates from Being.

I suspect the writer has been at the fount of Heidegger or some other continental luminary, drinking not wisely but too well. Is there no sense at all in this? Well, there is some sense in as much as I know that the writer is not talking about carpentry, flower-arranging or the political prospects for a common currency in Europe. It is not just gobble-degook. It does not consist of words randomly thrown together. But beyond this I have only a rough grasp. She is writing about the good performance of music. But I cannot imagine what would show me that what she says is true or false, and I have no idea how to set about checking whether, in a particular performance, cosmic affectivity is flowing from Being. Much writing about God is sober by comparison and its sobriety makes it easier to detect how language is being suborned, taken outside its normal sphere, and how it loses sense in the process. Compare the project, which mathematicians once pursued, of trying to square the circle. We now know that this is an impossibility. Did their description of their project have no sense because it involved an inconsistency? Well, we have a rough idea of what it might be appropriate to try to do. Equally, religious utterance is not total nonsense. There are things which it is proper to do in response to such talk and there are inferences which can be made from religious claims. Sense and nonsense, like the precise and imprecise, form a spectrum, and utterances range from one end to the other. They are not quite senseless or meaningless, but, fatally, religious utterances tend to fall towards the imprecise and senseless end of the spectrum.

There is, secondly, a stronger line of argument which I can advertise much more briefly. I shall show how, very often, putting moral qualities into a religious context distorts and despoils them. A religious framework fairly systematically corrupts morals.

2

Worship

In the first chapter I pointed out that our conception of God is the conception of somebody whom we worship and adore. To describe a very powerful being whom you do not worship, respect, love and regard as the standard of virtue is to describe something like a force of nature rather than a deity. Admittedly the gods of Greece and Rome were, on the whole, gods whom you worshipped out of fear rather than gods whom you loved, though, no doubt, religious practice was pretty varied in classical times and probably some worshippers had a similar attitude to their gods as we do to ours. But for modern man, God is to be worshipped with love, and the fear man has for God is of a different sort. It might be better described as 'awe'. The God of Christianity and Islam is merciful. We do not feel that we have to take steps to ward off the anger of God through various forms of propitiation.

So it is not surprising that worship is a central feature of religious practice. A glance through a hymn book shows an enormous preponderance of hymns expressing worship and adoration. Some of the greatest hymns express worship and gratitude. Addison's splendid hymn is typical of the sentiments they express, though it is superior to the usual run,

Worship

When all thy mercies, O my God,
My rising soul surveys,
Transported with the view, I'm lost
In wonder, love and praise.

Christians speak of Sunday worship. Indeed my impression is that for many Christians the act of worship is something far more important and central than the daily basis of trying to live well, without unkindness and malice, with charity and forbearance, though these matter, of course. The overwhelming importance of worship is reflected in the familiar opening words of the Shorter Catechism:

What is the chief end of man?
Man's chief end is, to glorify God and enjoy Him for ever.

Immediately, I think, we should find this strange and puzzling. 'End' presumably carries implications of the Aristotelian concept of telos; it is the idea of an end towards which we advance and in which we flourish. So it is essentially concerned with what is a good life to lead. We should not think, as we might initially be tempted to think, that what it means is that God has created us to provide a sort of band of cheer-leaders. Rather, what is involved is the idea that the end is a better state to be in, and that better state is one towards which we progress in so far as we live the life which is proper for us. So to live well is to live in such a way that eventually we shall reach the state of glorifying God and enjoying him for ever. So on any reasonable interpretation of this phrase it must mean that man flourishes when he glorifies and enjoys God. Two other points need to be considered. The good life does not end with this life; it projects into the future; in a later chapter I shall discuss whether an eternal life could be a good life to lead. Note, as well, that this is man's chief end and not the only end. We may have others. But these others will, presumably, be subordinate.

This last calls for a little reflection. I might have an ambition to run my own hairdressing salon. But, according to the Catechism, such an ambition should not be my chief end. Since my chief end is to glorify God whatever else I do *en route* ought to contribute to that. As George Herbert put it in a hymn I have already quoted:

> Teach me, my God and King,
> In all things Thee to see;
> And what I do in anything
> To do it as for Thee!
>
> All may of thee partake;
> Nothing can be so mean,
> Which with this tincture, 'for thy sake',
> Will not grow bright and clean.

Is there any reason to think this true? Why should not life possess a large number of quite independent purposes? It might be gratifying to find some sort of unity in our arrangements so that everything in the end contributes to one grand End but to me, as a non-believer, that this should be so seems something which would have to be taken on trust. I can see no unity within the purposes of wanting to finish the crossword, wanting to go for a swim, wanting to learn Spanish and wanting my children to be contented. Some of my purposes conflict. I do not have time both to work at philosophy and improve my piano-playing, much as I would like to do both. If I were a religious man might I not find that time spent working at my bench is time which I might otherwise spend in prayer and meditation? Moreover the suggestion that solving the crossword contributes to the greater glory of God looks utterly absurd.

A Christian might argue in reply that he glorifies God whenever he does something well. So he might feel he ought to do his best at anything he puts his hand to. But, pushed to its limits, this policy becomes rather foolish. There comes a point at which it is more sensible to give up than to waste further time on an essentially trivial enterprise such as this. If this is so, how can George Herbert reply to the objection that doing the crossword is bound to be time taken away from glorifying God? This is not a trivial or teasing question. I well remember a vicar telling me that whilst a missionary in South America he had remonstrated with evangelicals who took the view that time spent on medical treatment for the Indians was time which would be better spent saving souls. So not only is there no reason to suppose that there exists a grand overall unity in our purposes but also, and worse still, the attempt to produce one by cutting out unnecessary pursuits is liable to produce the sort of monomaniac who alarmed my vicar, a person who actually neglects his moral duties. In such a case religious commitment is all too obviously the enemy of morality.

There is a more important objection, and it is an objection which marks out something characteristic about religious morality. Once again I think it exemplifies the way that religious commitment taints our moral life. If I want, as I do, my children to be contented, that wish has nothing to do with my desire to see God glorified, and if it did, it would be soiled. Because I love my children and grandchildren, I want to see them flourish. Of course, I want to see many other people flourish who have nothing to do with me at all. I would like to see an end to war and want. If those desires were subservient to an overall aim, if I had them only because I thought that the satisfaction of those desires contributed to the glory of God, then there would be something gravely wrong. I want there to be an end to nationalist wars in Europe because I want there to be an end to human suffering. Any ulterior motive is not only irrelevant but also damages in implying that, without some further end, these purposes would not completely motivate us. I have met missionaries who justify their medical work on the grounds that it gives them an opportunity to get their message across, just as in some Salvation Army hostels down-and-outs could not get their soup until they had attended a service. But that we see suffering is a sufficient motive in itself to drive the purpose to put an end to it. Nothing else is needed, and the suggestion that another and higher order motive is required dilutes the original. Place the motive to relieve suffering in a religious context and you corrupt and despoil it by making it into a different and less worthy motive. As I have said, this is very characteristic of what happens when morality is given a religious cloak. Even if the believer says, as he might, that we have two good motives for reducing suffering, one moral and one religious, the fact remains that the moral motive ought to be sufficient. The religious motive is then either redundant or diminishing.

Now for the second difficulty: the claim that our chief end is to glorify God is, as I said, an odd claim. It implies that God has so created us that any independence we have of him is illusory in the sense that only by falling in with his aims for us can we flourish. Would it not have been more honourable of him to create beings who choose their own ends, sometimes succeeding and sometimes failing? Sometimes their reach is not equalled by their grasp, sometimes what they choose turns out to be unworthy, and sometimes they learn through hard experience what the best sort of life will be. Imagine, and this is an analogy which I shall repeatedly call upon, imagine a father who decides in advance what his daughter should do with her life and channels her into teaching or nursing or whatever. Do not we feel that this sort of direction of a child's life is insufferable? Of course, we all know of parents who have done this, often because they want their children to succeed where they feel that they themselves have failed. But a child with spirit will rebel.

In developing this second argument, I assume that the ways in which we describe God have their basis ultimately in human experience. But of course there are differences. What we do is to subtract the limitations and failings of our human models when speaking of God, and in doing this we assume that the resulting ways of talking have no cata-strophic defects. If my father loved me, then, through thinking of God as analogous to a human father in the required respects, I can speak of God as loving me. At the same time I assume that this shift has no consequences which are fatal to this way of talking. So we arrive at our conception of God's qualities in a pretty standard way. They are all produced by raising human qualities to another power. God is the Good Shepherd, the Father of Mankind, the Lord of all, etc. Philosophers and theologians have spilt much ink over the precise way in which this is done. Talk of analogy and metaphor is rife. In the first chapter I confessed to having severe misgivings about the propriety of this move. I believe that as we delve into the matter, we will find that because our ordinary non-theological language arises in from a specific human situation and is given sense by that context, if we then alter the context, it is by no means clear that what we are saying has meaning. Because I can say with perfect propriety that my father loved me, it does not follow that I can say with equal propriety that God loves me. (I shall return to the topic of love in a later chapter, but readers who want to pursue this general topic in more detail should look elsewhere, perhaps beginning with the many excellent companions to philosophy which have proliferated in the last decade. Most contain a reading list as well as a concise survey of popular positions.)

I voiced doubts about God so creating us that we only flourish in as much as we glorify him. Any earthly father who so circumscribed the life of his children would deserve our censure. Now why should the situation with God be any different? As I have said, Christians regularly and centrally speak of God as 'Our Father', so this is not an artificial problem. The obvious reply for a Christian to give is that because God's knowledge is not, like a human father's, imperfect, he always knows what is best for us. But this simply does not meet the point. It is not the imperfection of the human father's information which is the root of the problem. It is his desire to command. In one sense the theological case is worse, for God has either arranged the world in such a way that we flourish if we glorify him or made us such that we flourish if we glorify him. In either case he is made to sound like a rather more competent King Lear.

Thirdly, the Catechism uses the word 'glorify'. Following the same line of argument, we can start by asking what sort of person wants to be glorified or adored, or worshipped. I hope that you, the reader, do not want to be worshipped. Assuming that you are a half decent person and do not want to be worshipped, how would it be if you were very much more clever, good and powerful? Would you then want to be glorified, worshipped or adored? Even less so, I would have thought. If God is as good as he is made out to be, I cannot think that he would take any satisfaction in being worshipped or adored.

Nobody thinks to ask whether God wants to be worshipped. But apply the same method as we adopted in thinking of God as a father. Think of somebody who is mature and wise and try to magnify these gifts. Then ask yourself what characteristics it would be reasonable to credit him with. If you, the reader, are highly skilled in some department, say cabinet-making, would it give you any satisfaction to be complimented, lavishly, by somebody who has no understanding of what you do? Hardly. It would be merely irritating or embarrassing. It would be reasonable to be complimented by one's peers. For a young pianist to be complimented on his playing by Alfred Brendel would mean something. To be complimented by a member of the general public, nothing (though he might have been delighted to have given someone pleasure). By parity of reasoning, God, who exceeds all human capacities and merits, can hardly be pleased by the adulation of the uncomprehending.

What sort of individual would be gratified by having an audience of neighbours and hangers-on standing outside the house saying how wonderful he or she is? Well, we all know the answer to that question. It is those human figures who rightly disgust us, the Neros, Stalins, Maos, Napoleons and Saddam Husseins of this world who want or wanted to be idolized, who have massive monuments to their own glory put up and love the attentions of sycophants. They are or were objects of what we have come to call 'the cult of personality'. A Conservative minister recently observed that although he admired Margaret Thatcher, the stench of sycophancy around her revolted him. It is puzzling to ordinary decent people why anybody should desire this sort of adulation. It is not an admirable trait even if the person in question merits it, which in these cases they clearly do not. The shining eyes and uplifted faces of the party faithful as they deliver the standing ovation to the Leader at the party conference is something which most of us find disgusting. Why on earth should we think God desires adulation? We model God on the most appalling of human figures.

Sophisticated Christians will be dismissive of this third objection. They will argue that God wants us to praise him not because he likes it but because it is good for us. There are problems here as well. Is there any independent reason to think that it is good for us, evidence, perhaps, that people who spend hours adoring God turn out to be better people? No more reason than we have already found for thinking that people are morally better to the extent that they are deeply religious.

Still, on all these matters there is room for intelligent disagreement. The particular axe I am grinding is rather different. Worship or adoration are phases of moral development which go with the development of the self and the ideal self-image. The teenager needs role models, and it is natural for him to look up to older men or women who may or may not be well-known public figures, such as footballers or rock stars. It might be a bit strong to describe him as worshipping or adoring these people, but its kinship with these attitudes is pretty clear. Amongst religious people this attitude survives into adulthood. They replace the role models of adolescence with Jesus Christ or the Virgin Mary, figures whose feet of clay they will never see. To use a rather Freudian term, the concept of worship begins to look like a transference, a shift of a pattern of behaviour natural in the immature. Where it persists in adulthood it is a form of infantilism. Having exhausted earthly models, believers look to a Being who cannot disappoint their expectations.

I suggested that this smacks of immaturity. A man of forty who 'worships the ground his mother walks on' has not grown up. At that age he should love his mother but see her faults and forgive them. If a man 'worships' his wife you fear for his marriage. It is not so much that all human beings are tainted with vice, though no doubt they are. It is more the commonsense observation that the virtues we have are compensated for by parallel vices. Somebody who is utterly reliable and punctilious may be a bit dull. Somebody who is spontaneous and fun to be with may not be somebody with whom you would entrust your bottom dollar. The very considerate person may also irritate you by fussing over you. The woman whose criticism you find helpful on some occasions may be too prickly when you are sensitive. The man whose wit makes him marvellous company may also be cruel. The cruelty and the comedy go together. Do without one and you are liable to do without the other. So it goes on.

Let us pause for a moment; for the believer has a serious objection to the way I have developed this argument. It is that I have neglected one important aspect of the motive for worship and that is gratitude. The worship of God almost invariably involves thanking him. There is no question of immaturity involved here. To thank God for his mercies is natural and proper, and this marks out the adulation of God from the adulation of those human figures I mentioned. To quote again from one of the greatest of Anglican poets, George Herbert, after apostrophizing God as 'King of Glory, King of Peace', he continues:

> Thou hast granted my request,
> Thou hast heard me;
> Thou didst note my working breast,
> Thou hast spared me.

And it is interesting that those inadequate lusters after power who become our rulers often desire gratitude from their subjects though without usually having done anything for them. A particularly grisly piece of news film recently showed an aged man kissing the hands of a smiling Saddam Hussein.

Now there are two problems with this reply. The first is an obvious one which has been well worked over, and I do not intend to do more than just mention it. It is the very familiar problem of evil. Does it make sense to express gratitude to God when not only good comes to us out of the blue but also evil? I may feel gratitude to him that I have reached the age of sixty without major illness, but should I also feel angry with him that my father died prematurely? If 'my lines have been written in pleasant places', as my grandfather used to say, what about those wretched victims of civil war in Chechnya, Bosnia, Ethiopia and elsewhere? At this point gratitude begins to look monstrously egocentric. In expressing gratitude for my good luck, I also express, by implication, relief that I was not brought up in Ulster or the slums of London or Liverpool. For either God ordained these evils or he permits them. And as D.Z.Phillips has pointed out to me, the very business of trying to explain away suffering by saying that it is part of God's master plan seems to minimize in an inhuman way the actual suffering of people and animals. (He quoted with utter disgust the Irish priest who said to a family who had lost their five-year-old daughter, 'She's just taken an early bus'.)

Now this, what philosophers and theologians call a 'theodicy', is not something I intend to debate, though it is part of the background of my discussion. Rather, what I want to raise is a more complex and interesting question which often worries non-believers like myself. It is this. Can I have a secular conception of gratitude for those things which I have not earned and which have not been given me voluntarily by some individual? If I can, then the next step in my argument will be to show that that notion is somehow despoiled by giving it a divine context, in fact by turning it into worship.

There are some obvious differences between being grateful for a fine day and being grateful to somebody. To be simply grateful for a fine day, or for good health or for the ability to appreciate music, does not need to be weighed against the bad things, the rainy days, less intellectual ability than you might have had or a failure to love the visual arts. I write this on a beautiful summer's day in West Wales, a day which will end with my having a swim in the sea. But Welsh weather is frequently wet and depressing. Gloomy people will say to me 'We shall pay for this', as though God allocates the weather so that we all get some bad weather in the course of time. And if somebody does you a mixture of bad and good turns, it is reasonable enough to set gratitude against irritation. You might feel that the good turn is some sort of recompense. But thankfulness for good health, unearned and undeserved, for fine weather and a beautiful place, is unlike gratitude for the music of Joseph Haydn. I do not need to be grateful to somebody for this, as I am grateful to Haydn for what he left us. I just accept it and welcome it as it comes. To turn gratitude *simpliciter* into gratitude to God inevitably launches one off in the direction of a theodicy, a vindication of the justice of God's creating the world as he has. Turning gratitude into gratitude to God changes it, and the changes are morally relevant. Quite fundamentally we admire those people who are grateful for the good things in life and put up stoically with the bad. They do not draw up balance sheets over these matters. If they are optimistic, their optimism is unmotivated by any overmastering belief. So if, as I believe, worship is inextricably bound up with gratitude, then the conversion of ordinary gratitude into worship despoils a very central virtue in the best human beings. It turns the best aspects of stoicism into a calculation of gains and losses.

We are back on familiar ground. Worship implies gratitude; but gratitude, when constrained within worship, becomes gratitude to somebody. The ordinary thankfulness for what are matters of chance and fortune, which is probably something quite fundamental in human beings, becomes transmuted. What is interesting is that believers often sub-consciously see this in their responses. They praise and thank God for the good things. They do not blame him for what goes wrong. My point is that they can properly do this only in so far as they have some solution to the problem of evil. They have some deep conviction that God orders all for the best. As I said, ordinary gratitude becomes distorted by being turned into something different, a gratitude dependent upon a theodicy which, with the best will in the world, is debatable.

3

Faith and Trust

I

Philosophers have traditionally concentrated on the way in which we learn to distrust and doubt and have, as a matter of professional honour, encouraged the critical examination of belief. Pretty obviously, the Cartesian method of systematic doubt is a paradigm of this. What has been called 'foundationalism' in philosophy has been an attempt, in the tradition of Descartes, to show how we can base our claims to know on a basis which is secure, perhaps the basis of what we see and hear in sense-perception. But we reach this basis by a process of systematic doubting of anything which is open to doubt. From this, Cartesians believed, we can build up once again the systems of knowledge we have in the natural sciences, our physics, chemistry and biology, on a quite secure foundation beginning with records of observation. For reasons which I do not need to go into here, this project is widely deemed to have failed. Nevertheless, in as much as it achieved one aim, the inculcation of a critical attitude on the part of its students, its consequences are not all bad. Distrust, doubt, a critical attitude and the questioning of what seems obviously true are all essential parts of philosophical method and it is hard to imagine philosophy without them.

Faith and Trust

What philosophers in that tradition were not interested in is the attitude of trust. They tended to dismiss it, if they ever thought about it at all, as pre-critical and something altogether to be regretted. Trust is what peasants have in the teaching of the church, fundamentalists in the Bible and the followers of 'alternate' systems of belief like astrology, paganism, new age religion have in the various sorts of nonsense believed by the perusers of the bookshelves in wholefood shops. Still, we can agree with philosophers that uncritical acceptance is something we should learn to reject and still think that the notion of trust is worth investigating and that trust, in its various forms, has a central role in everybody's life. Wittgenstein's later work has, more than anything else, brought the notion of trust to our attention. It will be no news to the reader that trust, too, is a very important feature of the Christian religion. A glance through the Bible reveals how often its writers talk about trust in God, or, in the New Testament, faith in God. Trust and faith, though not identical, are certainly closely related. But we must begin by thinking over the various ways in which we use the word 'trust'. As we shall see, there are several quite distinct varieties of trust.

Think of a small child. A child who is just beginning to learn to talk 'naturally' trusts her parents; obviously, she trusts her parents to care for her; what they give her to eat and drink she eats and drinks; as an infant her bond with her mother is unlearnt; she does not and cannot consider whether mother's milk is good for her and take it on that basis. Her father is around and she 'naturally' trusts him to take care of her. Wittgenstein suggests that the child's acquisition of language is dependent upon this trust. As the child takes what she is given, so she learns a vocabulary in the same way, and her earliest attempts at sentences are corrected and expanded by her parents. 'Cat' means cat and it does not occur to her to question this. As Wittgenstein remarks, belief must precede doubt. So she imitates those who speak to her, believing what they say, acquiring her language without ever considering whether she is being taught correctly. That question does not arise. Her acquisition of her native tongue is an outgrowth of an attitude of trust which is exemplified in all sorts of other areas, her trust that she will not be dropped when she is carried, that her parents can 'make it better' when she falls and so on.

Childlike trust is thus an implicit and unquestioning attitude to others. Some children are shy of strangers; others regularly display trust with people outside their family circle. But any child who did not show trust to her parents would face huge problems. A very important facet of this, which Wittgenstein did not remark upon as far as I know, is that there is no context for this trust. The young child trusts her parents implicitly in everything, from what she eats and drinks to what they say. The context may be limited in that she does not trust strangers, but within a family group trust is normally contextless. In this way it is unlike the forms of trust which are most familiar in adult life. I trust the man who looks after my cars because I have learnt from experience that he is reliable, honest and does not overcharge me. So my trust has a context. If I am asked whether I would trust him to advise me on investments, I would say 'no'. He might know about such things, he might not. But I have no reason to suppose that he does. People who know me might say that I am trustworthy; but the context is important; they trust me to be careful in reading other people's work and giving an opinion on it because they have found that I am reliable in these matters. My students know that whilst I can usually be relied upon to turn up at the right time for the beginning of a new course of lectures, I cannot be relied upon to turn up at the right lecture room. (On one occasion, the first year class ran a book on it.) Asked, do I trust my wife?, I will reply 'Of course'. I trust her to call me if she has promised, not to go off with the travelling circus which comes through Wales from time to time and not to get us into financial difficulties. But I do not trust her sense of direction and I do not trust her to find her way back to the car if she has parked it in a strange city. Such trust is based on experience. We find out who can be relied upon and on what matters they are reliable. And the fact is that all of us are unreliable about some things. On some matters our judgment is poor. If we know ourselves well, then we recognize where we are untrustworthy and warn other people off. The problems arise when we have misplaced confidence in our own judgment.

So as a child grows up, she develops the experience which turns the initial, uncritical and natural trust into a trust which depends on experience and in which such experience provides a context for the trust. She discovers that her father's political judgment is eccentrically unreliable and that her mother's religious beliefs are simplistic and contradictory. She learns not to trust what her father says about politics and her mother says about religion. But she might trust both of them when they advise her against making too close a friend of Jane, whose mother's boy-friend has done time. So trust turns into something which is rationally assessed and for which there are grounds.

But trust can take other forms. Sometimes I decide to trust somebody else without having any grounds for doing so.

The Moral Case against Religious Belief

Supposing somebody calls at the door asking to borrow a jack to change a wheel. You lend him one. You know he might drive off with it but you take a chance. This form of trust is neither childlike trust nor based on a rational assessment of reliability and, unlike the first two, it has moral implications. You act this way because to act differently would demean you. It would be mean-spirited to ask him to leave you a deposit. There is a grace in risking your own well-being rather than mistrusting a stranger. It is sad if you think you have been made a fool of when somebody cheats you. Kierkegaard wrote:

> It mortifies our vanity and our pride to have thought too well of a swindler, to have been foolish enough to have believed him – for it is a contest between brain and brain. One is vexed at oneself, or at least one finds that it is . . . 'so stupid' to have been fooled. But ought it not to seem equally stupid to us, to say the least, to have believed evil, or suspiciously to have believed nothing, when there was good! . . . But here in the world it is not 'stupid' to believe evil of a good man, it is a superciliousness by which one adroitly gets rid of the good; but it is 'stupid' to think well of an evil man.

Another similar case: should you give a lift to a hitch-hiker? Most of us have been in this particular quandary. There is a risk, of course, but it is small. It is a greater risk for a young woman than for a large man. To take the risk is to act well, though we will not judge harshly the nervous man who does not stop. In a slightly different vein you might give money to a beggar, trusting that he would spend it on the food he obviously needs and not a bottle of cheap cider. It is prudent to do this in small ways, but not to entrust somebody with large sums of money. This is not merely because you would waste your assets if you gave him hundreds of pounds; it is also because such sums might be better disposed of elsewhere. If you are to give away large sums of money it might be better to ensure that the money will be well used.

Now another sort of trust. A woman's car breaks down miles from anywhere at night. A passing motorist stops to help. Her trust in him is, let us assume, Hobson's choice. He might just be the local mad axe-man, but this is improbable. She takes a chance because there is no alternative, and in that respect the case is different from the previous. It is a rational decision in the circumstances. Her trust in him is motivated by the fact that no other option is left open to her. It is also unlike the previous case in having no comparable moral content. She does not act either well or badly in acting this way and it is not good of her to trust the passer-by.

Finally a fifth and, I think, somewhat complex and controversial case. We are unsurprised when a man trusts his wife or a father his son in circumstances where another would not. Thirty or forty years ago, in the neighbourhood in which I then lived, a young man emigrated to Canada. Not much was heard of him for three or four years and there was complete silence for two years, during which it was rumoured that he was in prison. His mother and father, working-class people, had bought their own terraced house in the meantime. He returned and persuaded them to put up their house as security for a garage business which he was starting. He assured them there was no risk. The business failed, the house was sold and the parents spent the rest of their lives in a caravan park. His father, in particular, was shattered by the events and died quite soon. What do you think about the behaviour of the parents? Do you think they were crazy to entrust their house to their son? Or do you think, as I am inclined to do, that it is understandable and, in a way, admirable, that they trusted their son where nobody else would? They assumed, I think, that a son would do nothing to harm his elderly parents. No doubt, like many people who live on the edge of the law, he was feckless and foolishly over-confident about what he could achieve and probably extravagant when money came his way. Probably he did not intend to risk their money and, in that way, their judgment was right. He was imprudent and unable to take a long view rather than malicious. Where they were wrong was in trusting his judgment. Obviously it would have been better had they not allowed him to commit their house as security and nobody would have blamed them had they refused. And yet we have an admiration for somebody who trusts those he loves even where that trust is imprudent. The thought 'My son cannot do that to me' describes a sort of trust which is neither childlike, nor a calculated assessment of reliability, nor a deliberate decision to take a chance; nor is it trust where there is no alternative. It invites and often ends in self-deception, of course, but its role in our lives is not to be minimized, and it has implications for the sorts of beings we are and the sorts of life which we think are good lives. For we must be more ready to countenance evidence which counts against the trustworthiness of relative strangers or a casual acquaintance, than we would of a close friend or somebody we love. It is proper, and it is not irrational to stick up for those who are close to you.

This comes out in another way. Ask yourself when and where reasons are appropriate for trusting somebody. If a woman gave reasons why she trusted her husband not to be unfaithful we would think that there was something wrong. It would not be a proper marriage relationship. If she were to say 'he is so exhausted after I have finished with him that he is incapable of playing fast and loose with somebody else', we might not be very convinced of the depth of their relationship.

So I have distinguished five sorts of trust. Now we might be tempted to think that it is virtuous to be trusting, but the distinctions I have made complicate this somewhat. The child's trust in her parents is neither virtuous nor vicious. It is a fact of nature. My prudent reliance on somebody I have found that I can trust does not reflect either well or badly on me, nor is there anything virtuous in the woman motorist's decision to trust the stranger who offers to help. She has no alternative. This leaves two categories in which trust might be thought to be a virtue. The first is where I trust in somebody knowing that I take a risk. As I write, the newspapers are full of the story of an Anfield vicar who, knowingly, worked with people who were dangerous and was murdered as a result. Even if we think he was imprudent, we admire this man deeply. His preparedness to work with and trust people whom others would not trust and who, in this case, abused his trust, shows courage and selflessness. Our admiration is, I think, magnified by the recognition that he took seriously the demands of his beliefs and put his own life on the line.

The second case is the final case of the man who trusted, unwisely, his son where nobody else would. We may think that this trust reflects well on the father; that he was virtuous in trusting his son. To trust those you love in this way is part of what it is to lead a good life.

II

So which of these forms of trust is the model for the believer's talk of trust in God? Believers often speak of a childlike trust or a childlike faith as though that is admirable. The idea of a God as a father encourages such an attitude. But if our faith in God is a childlike trust, then there is something distinctly odd about it. Obviously it is unlike a child's trust, primarily because adult believers are not children. It is not a phase in a development which ends with our making distinctions as to whom and on what matters we can trust. It does not eventually lead to a situation where we find we can trust God on some things and not on others. It never ends with our finding a context for trust. We do not find that God can be trusted to forgive us but not to help us to win the lottery. And when an adult shows a childlike trust it is not a virtue. We care for those of restricted mental growth and perhaps love them because they are innocent, but we do not think theirs is a state to be coveted.

Neither of the two forms of trust which I did grant to be morally admirable are cases which can provide a model for the believer's trust in God. It makes no sense to speak of me entrusting God with my small change when I give it to the church collection, hoping that he won't do something noxious with it. If I cast myself upon God, not knowing what he will do with my life, only the religious heretic would say that he might do something terrible with it which ends with my destruction. I take no risks. Religious orthodoxy claims that God orders things for the best. If dedicating my life to God ends with my being stabbed in a Liverpool churchyard, this is reckoned to be part of God's overall plan. This holds equally if we consider modelling trust in

God on the father's trust in his erring son. For again we are assured that ultimately, taking the next life into consideration, there are no risks for the man who trusts God. God will not let him down as a human being may let him down. Once again a theodicy intervenes and once again its effect is to transmute trust into something which no longer has the moral dimension it had before. It turns trust into reliance. If I trust God with my life I take no chances, for the theodicy tells me that God orders everything for the best. The sort of trust that really is a virtue ceases to be a virtue when put into a theological context.

Is there then any alternative to construing trust in God on the model of childlike trust? As I have said (and our rejection of the two cases where trust is a virtue emphasizes this), trust in God is contextless. God is to be trusted on everything and the questioning of God's goodness or power in those moments of doubt which come to nearly every believer is not like my having momentary doubts about the wisdom of the Chancellor of the Exchequer. No experience in this life will show either that God ought or ought not to be trusted. We experience good and evil, joy and pain; taken at face value nothing suggests a supreme director of the universe who cares for us. For that we need the leap of faith, and the leap of faith gives us a trust which is contextless, like the trust of the infant.

Trust in God, I conclude, is not a virtue. Men do not live well through trusting in God. In most cases trust in God is nothing more than an idly spinning wheel, as Wittgenstein would have put it, a faith which has no part in life beyond the rituals of the religious life. I suppose that it means that believers will meet disaster with acceptance and resignation and, ultimately, an optimism about the future. But it cannot make any difference to those areas of our life where trust does have a moral dimension. For the rest of our life, we must go on making decisions about who and where to trust as before. More relevantly, we have to make decisions about risk, and the risks we are prepared to take are central to the sort of moral life we lead. We show the moral life we live essentially in the way we trust others in contexts where there is a risk. This shows the stuff we are made of. Of course, to be trustworthy is a virtue, but that is another matter. As far as trust in God is concerned it is just another instance of the way in which a concept, namely childlike trust, which describes a natural, important and transient feature of our lives, is dragged out of its normal setting and illicitly given a role in adult life in which it is manifestly out of place. For adults to display childlike trust suggests arrested development.

Sentimentalists about religion think that the innocence of childhood is superior to the moral complexity of the adult life. Of course it distorts a central feature of the Christian tradition to think this way. With all the faults of men and women, God chose to give them the power to do right and wrong, and that marks a different order and an order not inferior to that of innocence. It is crystallized in the paradox of the Fortunate Fall. The Fall of Man meant that human beings would become fuller moral agents, free makers of decisions for good and evil. They were no longer children. Wittgenstein's celebration of the trust shown in confession in which one becomes 'as a little child' reveals that rather unappetizing sentimentality which was liable to come over him when he thought about religion.

To end let us briefly consider the rather alarming story of Abraham and Isaac. Remember that God told Abraham to take his only son and sacrifice him for a burnt offering. But at the moment when Abraham was about to cut his son's throat, an angel intervened. It was now clear that Abraham feared God, and his preparedness to kill the son he loved would be rewarded by the blessing of his descendants. What I see this as illustrating, and what it clearly was not intended to illustrate, is both the naturalness of trust and its limits. Naturally Isaac trusted his father, and we are supposed to take the trust that Abraham shows in God as mirroring the trust Isaac has in his father. But there is something disturbing about a father who is prepared, even supposing he knows that it is God who is telling him what to do, to sacrifice his child. Abraham shows himself to be the dupe of his own trusting nature and Jehovah shows himself prepared to abuse Abraham's trust in order to make a point. An adult trusts and risks – but not in this way (and do not say that trust in God can never be betrayed; that is not the point).

Trust is cognate with faith, one of the three theological virtues, the others being hope and charity. What we now see is that the form of trust that believers have in God lacks even that feature which makes the trust of small children necessary to their development, namely that it is something which they outgrow. Once again religious belief takes a feature necessary to human life out of context, immobilizes it and turns it into something which no longer has the function it once had.

For child-like trust to occur outside its normal setting (which is childhood) is pernicious, as disgusting as the behaviour of a precocious child. It is exploited by various unsavoury characters such as many popes, ayatollahs and the leaders of charismatic and millennialist sects who trade on the fact that most of us have no access to what God says other than what somebody says he says. Trust is, after all, deeply implicated in the most extreme forms of human wickedness and misery precisely through the fact that to trust God also involves trusting somebody who claims to speak on behalf of God. People trust God because human beings have told them to trust God. These same human beings tell them what God's plans and wishes for the world are. Even if they all told us the same thing that would be no reason to suppose they accurately reflect what God has decided. Since they tell us different things, we ought to be sceptical. How could anybody think that in an adult childlike trust is a virtue?

4

Love

I

A very little reflection shows us that the English word 'love' gives us a somewhat impoverished conception of love. We use it mainly to express love between parents and children and to express sexual love (of which I shall speak in the next chapter). We no longer use it very much to describe or express the love between friends which earlier generations thought so important. The relationship between David and Jonathan is a relationship which we would nowadays assume to be gay, though I presume it was not. We no longer speak of non-sexual love between men. Earlier generations of English speakers could use the word 'charity' to express a sort of fellow feeling, a sense which is preserved in our word 'uncharitable'. We see it in St. Paul's famous paean in I Corinthians:

Though I speak with the tongues of men and angels, and have not charity, I am become as sounding brass, or a tinkling cymbal.
And though I have the gift of prophecy, and understand all mysteries, and all knowledge; and though I have all

faith, so that I could remove mountains, and have not charity, I am nothing.

Charity suffereth long, and is kind; charity envieth not; charity vaunteth not itself and is not puffed up.

But for modern English speakers charity has become synonymous with alms-giving. Of course, we also use 'love' to describe our affection for other animate and inanimate objects. 'He loves his garden', 'She loves the music of Elgar', 'Gerald loves cooking' and 'Jenny loves horses'. But by comparison with Greek or Arabic, English is poor in words to describe the varieties of love. On the face of it this may not seem such a loss. We can do what I shall begin by doing, make the necessary distinctions by qualifying the word 'love'. But where we do not have a word in our vocabulary the idea does not naturally occur to us. I ought to be able to say that I love some of my colleagues without implying a homosexual or heterosexual attachment. What we cannot easily express in words without circumlocution we may be inhibited from feeling; perhaps we will even misclassify that form of emotion when it does occur. For what emotions we suffer depend in part upon the resources in our language for expressing them. Because we think of love as, primarily, romantic love we look for romantic love in our lives, welcome it and nurture it, and so our lives change as a result. It is very important to us in our culture that we experience this sort of love, and we tend to think of love as a special sort of feeling. So very many romantic ballads and popular songs emphasize this. As a consequence, other important aspects of love become less significant to us. We emphasize feeling a special warmth for the other at the expense of maintaining a committed permanent relationship of mutual caring, for example. On the other hand, constricted by this model of what love is, I may not see that my affection for a friend of the same sex should be counted as love. As a consequence, I fail to see the nature of the tie between us. I fail to see how deeply I care about him. But what I do not see I do not act upon, and since, to a large extent, the relationship between us is made up of the ways we behave to each other, my failure to act in a loving way ends up by my changing the sort of relationship we have. For example, it is commonly said that men do not talk to each other about how they feel as freely as they should. If this is true, and I suspect there is something in it, it probably has something to do with the fact that only a gay man can speak of loving another man. If men could say that some of their friendships were friendships which amounted to love they could talk to each other about intimate matters which they now cannot. You can then see that a limited recognition of the forms of love between human beings means a limitation on the forms of love we experience and express. So it is not as though our vocabulary does not matter. We ought not to be tempted into thinking that on the one hand we have human relationships and on the other hand we have the ways of describing them and that the first will go on independently of the second. It is not at all like describing the physical world. If we have no names and no classification for the majority of Australian flowers, the flowers will go on blooming nonetheless. But it does not follow that human emotions for which we have no names will go on blossoming in their despite.

Left with the deficiencies of English, we can do little but try to make distinctions where they are necessary. Observation, attention and insight are required for us to see that the description of our relationship to others is not completely catered for in the existing classification. It needs work. Of course, for many forms of love, the distinctions are obvious and we are at no risk of being confused. I shall assume that I can say that I love my wife, my children, my mother, my friends, Samuel Johnson, cricket, sunny weather, the beach and a bottle of Sancerre and assume that the implications are different for each case. Equally, when a believer says she loves God, certain behaviour is proper, and that behaviour enables us to see the difference between loving God and loving her child.

II

So what about our love for God? Religious believers say that they love God. The writer of Deuteronomy (or one of them) enjoins us to love God. 'Thou shalt love the Lord thy God with all thy heart, with all thy soul and with all thy might' (Deut. 6.5). Can they love God?

The initial question must be on what other forms of human love the love of God might be modelled. For once again, we have to start with the human situation and move to an exposition of how such terms apply to God. There is no alternative. Perhaps the problem is easier to understand where we speak, not of our love for God but of God's love for us. In this case we do not first have an experience of God's love which we then extend to our parents. Rather, we experience the love and care of our parents for us and then learn how we can speak of God's love for us. It is crucially important to remember that this is how God's love is explained to a child. We always, without exception, begin with the familiar human situation. Now set aside the question as to how God might be said to love us. That brings us too quickly to the problem of evil, the problem of how a good God could have created a world with so much suffering; as I have said repeatedly, the question of justifying the evil in the world, what theologians and philosophers of religion call a 'theodicy', is a question I am not concerned with here. Rather, I am concerned with the other issue, our love for God; necessarily, as we see, the argument moves in the same way. Having experienced loving other humans we are encouraged to love God initially in the same way, whilst making allowances for the changed context.

So on what human forms could this love be modelled?

My mother used to say of somebody for whom she felt compassion that 'her heart went out to him'. It is a telling phrase which also might express that sudden welling up of affection for somebody or something you love, a warmth towards a place or to home, or to a favourite hymn. But more is expected of love than this. If you love somebody you will value them and you will do things for them. Love is not just a feeling. To love somebody is to want to do something for them.

Contrast this with the love of objects. My loving a building such as Gloucester Cathedral might involve wanting to see it often and also, it might imply, though it does not necessarily, that I try to get others to share my love and awe. Having found it a stunning experience I want other people to experience it as well. Not everybody feels like this. Obviously, some people, some collectors of art, for example, want to keep what they value to themselves and not to allow others to enjoy it. This strikes me as mean-spirited and is, fortunately, less of a possibility with arts like music, architecture and literature. There are some things we can do for architecture and the arts; if we love Gloucester Cathedral we will contribute to an appeal to maintain the fabric. If I love the music of Thomas Tallis, I will try to ensure by my patronage that it continues to be performed. But these ways of acting in the interests of a building or some music are somewhat limited.

But what is present in the love we have for other human beings and is not normally present in the love we have for inanimate objects is that we have certain ties of obligation and care. The people we love have needs, and these are needs which we are under a moral obligation to meet. In this respect our ties to persons are different. I am not bound to contribute to the cathedral appeal fund, but I am bound to care for my children. Since I love my children, I am concerned for their welfare and that means that I am concerned for their well-being. They matter to me.

So love is not just a feeling of warmth. There is more. If it is only a feeling of cosiness it is mere sentimentality. The difference comes out clearly in our relationship to animals. Think of some pet owners you know. Think of cases where a woman loves her cat or dog. There are some who want a cat or a dog to cuddle and who often lose interest in the pet very quickly after the initial excitement. They do not have the long-term interests of the animals at the forefront of their attention. The animal is an instrument for them. It is a means of indulging certain feelings. Others more properly view the animal as having its own interests. It needs affection but it also needs to be kept healthy and not over-indulged on sweets. A dog needs a walk, even when the weather is inclement, so a walk it must have.

Perhaps now my problem is becoming clear. How does

the religious believer prevent her love for God collapsing into a sort of sentimentality? She can only do this in so far as she can 'do things for God', but what does God want her to do for him? To act from love of God must be to do what is in God's interests. But what would that be?

Two view are possible here. The first is that I cannot have any obligations to God because God has no needs. That makes the situation radically different from the standard situation. The other is that we are somehow co-workers with God and assist him in his plans for the world. On the second picture, what does he require of us? The obvious answer to this is to follow Judaeo-Christian tradition and say that God wants three things of us: firstly to worship him, secondly to enlarge his kingdom by proselytizing and thirdly to act morally. We considered the first in the previous chapter and found difficulties with the notion of worshipping God. The second is not, in fact, a separate consideration. We proselytize in order to make converts who will do what? They will worship and love God. So the basis for converting the heathen, the motivation, has to be found in what loving and worshipping God involves. Making converts is not an end in itself, whilst acting rightly is. So we can ignore the second consideration and turn directly to the third: God also wants us to act well. This is central to a moral faith like Christianity. The problem is that the Christian tradition is not unambiguous on what constitutes acting well. On the one hand we have the marvellous words of Zechariah,

> Thus speaketh the Lord of hosts, saying, 'Execute true judgment, and shew mercy and compassion every man to his brother;

And oppress not the widow, nor the fatherless, the stranger, nor the poor' (Zech. 7. 9–10).

No mention here of monkish virtues, of perpetual virginity, of obedience to superiors in the church, of scourging oneself, of spending a lifetime on top of a pedestal, of ensuring nothing is placed on top of the Holy Bible or of not playing football on Sundays, to take a random sample of the strange behaviour with which people think God might be pleased.

So the problem will now, I think, be obvious. Many of the things which Christians have thought God required of them are so bizarre, when they are not wicked, that it defies common sense that a deity should want human beings to act this way. Is it remotely conceivable that God should be interested in whether people use a condom rather than the rhythm method as a means of contraception? If he does think the former is a sin then he seems to have lost all sense of proportion. The list of requirements I gave in the previous paragraph hardly count as moral requirements. To suppose that God prefers chastity, as successive Popes have declared, puts him in the position of a father who, having given his children sweets, asks them not to eat them as a way of showing their love for him. Now we know some earthly parents act this way and we rightly view them with contempt. A God who acted this way would be capricious, frivolous and self-centred to the point of unkindness. It is a picture of a Being it is impossible to admire, let alone love. What reason could we have for supposing that God requires abstinence which is half so certain as the fact that, for many people, it is physically and psychologically damaging, and thus an evil?

But turn back to the words of Zechariah and we see a now familiar pattern emerging. We need no further motivation to care for the poor, the widow, the fatherless and the stranger. That God requires it of us either turns it into something which is no longer moral but a matter of expediency, it being sensible to keep in with the Almighty, or else it dilutes the moral motivation. Either way it is a move for the worse.

I conclude, then, that it is hard to see how loving God can require of us the sort of behaviour which would give content to the idea of loving God. It leaves our love of God as a mere outpouring of emotion directed at a Being who is non-existent, as mere sentimentality in fact.

III

I have left until now an issue which many readers might think quite fundamental. Is there any sense in speaking of loving God at all? We might object that the context is such that it is extremely unclear whether believers can be said to love God given that their relationship to him is intrinsically different from their relationship with a friend whom they meet regularly in the body, who replies audibly to their remarks, whom they can hug or become cross with when she is irritable. After all the fact that God is a spirit rather alters matters. (We are told to worship him in spirit.) We might argue that, deprived of its normal context, it is uncertain whether there is any sense in the claim that I love God. I am not, however, going to pursue this path. Rather, I feel inclined to accept that believers love God. As we have seen, the objects of love can be very various. Certainly it seems that one could love somebody who does not exist. A child might love Santa Claus just as she fears the bogeyman. Generations of Christians feared witches, warlocks and Beelzebub. I don't know whether you, the reader, believe in angels. Some Christians do not. If you agree with me that angels, like the cherubim and seraphim, are inventions much as Tritons and the Great God Pan were inventions, you probably will not disagree with me in saying that less sophisticated Christians might love their guardian angels even though these beings do not exist. So I have no special difficulties in allowing that I can love somebody whom I have never seen and whose character is transmitted to me only via very old and very untrustworthy accounts of an earthly incarnation. (I am assuming that even if a defensible account of religious experience can be given, it will not disclose much of the deity; even Moses only saw a bit of Jehovah's bottom.)

It is less problematic still to allow that one can love somebody with whom one is not personally acquainted. Might I love Joseph Haydn or Samuel Johnson and did, perhaps, millions love Mahatma Gandhi who never knew or saw him? We are probably right to think of the Queen Mother as a much-loved figure. But perhaps a better analogy for religious attachment is the pop star or screen idol. Thousands of people loved or worshipped Elvis Presley. They never met him. But they plastered their rooms with his picture, with memorabilia, and sent flowers to his funeral. The ritual is remarkably similar to that in religious homes where icons of the Virgin Mary are to be found. Like the admirers of Elvis, the admirers of the Virgin Mary have never met her. There are, of course, some differences. We don't have any records of the Virgin Mary singing and she made no films. Her devotees know less about her than Elvis fans know about Elvis; of course, they pray to her, but if she replies in audible tones, this is not regarded as good news for the family and friends of the devotee.

Probably the next problem is now evident. The parallel which is closest to somebody's love of Christ, God or the Virgin Mary, namely the idolization of a public figure, does not square with other aspects of the love Christians say they have for God. The sort of love Christians and probably members of other religions think they have for God is much more like the love which I have for my wife, in whose company I constantly am. Christians look forward to being in the company of God for eternity. There is no suggestion this might be boring for either party, that God might sometimes want a change from being praised or that I might want to hear the other point of view from Satan. No, this is a permanent settlement of me on God and vice versa. Imagine carrying on a courtship by one-way correspondence and then passing directly to married life with no intervening spell! Once again our ordinary conceptions of a loving relationship are becoming remarkably stretched.

Suppose we can overcome these difficulties, which believers will probably think facetious, more serious difficulties lie in wait. What is a good loving relationship between two partners like? For a start it requires mutual adaptation. Sometimes one humours the other, sometimes one teases. You know when not to press the other; you recognize when the other is insecure and needs attention. Most couples have private jokes and pet names. I invite you to fill out the picture. It is because one partner is forgetful, incompetent at household repairs and is a bad driver whilst the other has a passion for soap operas and is liable to fits of extreme temper at the sight or sound of a political leader that we have the context in which relationships form as they do. They are not pure relationships between contextless abstract spirits. The more you fill out the context of the relationship, the more individual it seems and the more dependent upon a life in this world. There is a constant disparity between the models and paradigms on which religious talk depends and its application to God. God does not modify. His character is settled, whereas it is of the nature of human relationships that they change the two people concerned through mutual adaptation and mutual tolerance. But though I may change, God does not. 'With him there is no variableness nor shadow of turning' (James 1.17). Indeed orthodoxy says the revelation is final and we have no more to learn in this life about his character than what the church and the Bible possess. Unlike the Delphic oracle, God has no more to say.

I have sketched the form a good mature relationship develops. I can hardly have this with God. God does not adapt, and I adapt to him by becoming more rigid. To accustom myself to his immutability is to become more inflexible; by contrast, good relationships between human beings are a mixture of dependency and flexibility, yet without so much predictability as to be boring. My relationship to God can be more plausibly construed as that between a pet and the pet owner. It is like the relationship of a cat to his owner, all the time trusting that it will develop into the sort of relationship a master has with his spaniel.

My brief has been to attack the cogency of the religious view of a moral life. I have, inevitably given my background and culture, aimed at Christianity. Nevertheless, I believe that

Christianity did get something crucially right about what it is to live a good life, and that is that it made love central. I do not say that other religions did not get the same thing right. I don't know. I speak as a post-Christian and not as post-Jew or post-Muslim. I imagine there are traditions in other faiths which maintain similar doctrines. And, indeed, I believe that love, goodness and any happiness which is attainable are all interlinked. It is easier for somebody who is happy to be good, and goodness means acting to others through love.

But the love which Christianity enjoins is a universal love. It is a love for other people as well as God. Christ's words were that we must love our neighbour as ourself. The assumption is that pure love ought to be undifferentiated, and Christ had hard words for those who put family obligations before the needs of the cause. In the terminology of contemporary moral theory, Christ is an impartialist. He does not think that we have special obligations to our nearest and dearest. We ought rather to view the needs of others in an impartial way and meet them on the principles of abstract justice. But stop and consider what love is like. You have an affection for your own, for your husband, wife or partner, for your children, for your parents and then for your other relatives and friends. It is to them that your first obligation lies. The circles of concern spread outwards, wider and wider, like those from a stone thrown into a pond, becoming fainter all the while. Sometimes we are somewhat shocked and taken aback when the death of a pet occasions so much grief. 'It was only an animal', we say to ourselves, and reflect on the much greater suffering of those dying needlessly in civil wars in central Africa. For these innocent victims our compassion is temporary and not so deep. We might not feel, like Jane Austen, that it is fortunate that the victims are so little known to us and so far away, but it is a fact that an animal with whom we have spent a deal of our life matters more to us than the life of a child we never knew. Quite what one says to the couple who erected a memorial to their guinea-pig inscribed 'So brave, so good', I do not know, but they evidently grieved. But there is no point in regretting the partiality of our moral life. I am not convinced that things could be different, given the people we are. Grief requires a personal loss. Somebody who grieved as much about the death of a child in Burundi as he did about the death of his wife would appear to be some sort of monster.

So what is the upshot? I suggest that love for God is so unlike the standard cases of love that it comes to little more than a mere outpouring of warmth to a Being of whom our experience is at best controversial. It is sentimentality. I do not deny that believers love God. The problem is that the only forms of behaviour which would give body to the notion of love here are forms in which we can no longer have confidence, or else they already have sufficient motivation. The rituals of worship are increasingly *passé*; and as for silence, abstaining from sex, pilgrimages, flagellation and other ways of mortifying the flesh, it is impossible to imagine that a good God could want them. No decent father would want his children to show him how much they loved him by indulging in these practices; they are never good in themselves, they are sometimes bad and they are occasionally perverted; they seem more appropriate to propitiating a Being of uncertain temper. Perhaps they fit in with a God worshipped by Ulster Protestants and Serbian Orthodox, but they are ludicrously out of joint with a Being who embodies modern moral ideals. And what the love of God demands of us in the form of decent behaviour is already required of us by common-or-garden morality.

5

Sexual Love

The moral injunctions you recognize will depend to some extent on what you think of as a good life to lead. As you will now be clear, I believe that, in some respects, the Christian life is not a good life to lead. It requires Christians to act in ways which inhibit the flourishing of their lives. No philosophical critic was more trenchant in pointing this out than Nietzsche, and in the next chapter my criticism of the desirability of immortality will reflect some of the objections he made. The other area where the church seems to get things very seriously wrong is in the area of sexual morality. So in this chapter my objections to Christian belief are perhaps more objections of detail and substance than they have been so far. Up to this point I have concentrated on the way in which ideas like worship, gratitude and love, notions which play a central role in the Christian vision of the good life, become impoverished or distorted when they are applied to God. My conclusion has been that the moral life is despoiled rather than enriched by a religious setting. I have not suggested that what the churches typically advise is ever morally wrong. But when it comes to sexual morality, the churches, and in particular the Roman Church are guilty of advocating immoral doctrines.

As I remarked at the start, even non-believers are hesitant

in attacking the morality of the Christian view of sex and marriage. Though many people nowadays assume that the church's line on, say, contraception does not apply to them, they seem to assume that to obey it is an option for a moral agent. Although it may not be morally wrong to disobey the church, nevertheless it is not morally wrong to obey it. The general view seems to be that this is a neutral question. So whilst Roman Catholics who follow that teaching may be irrational, they are not wrong. I begin with the Christian conception of marriage, partly because the churches have a proprietary attitude to marriage, believing that they provide an ideal which non-believers cannot attain.

I suppose that one thing which ought to strike us immediately is the great variety in human relationships. Marriages certainly vary. We are accustomed to the thought that human beings differ as individuals, indeed that is a cliché, and we think this diversity is something to be valued, something which racism, *inter alia*, denies. Human beings vary widely, and any class or race contains both the stupid and the imaginative, the quarrelsome and the forgiving, the noble and the resentful.

It ought to be obvious that a corollary of this is that relationships between people are likely to vary. For if they were to be similar it would only be on the basis of some common denominator. But the difference between a deep relationship and a shallow one is precisely the fact that the former answers to the specific rather than the general in the individual. In as much as I see, value and respond to the specific qualities of my friend, then my relationship deepens from being just a matter of common manners and etiquette to something more profound.

The Moral Case against Religious Belief

The point about this preamble is that it is a mistake to suppose that there can be a basic ideal pattern of marriage; indeed to suppose that there can be moral patterns at all smacks of immaturity. Earlier I expressed doubts as to whether the moral life can properly be thought of as a set of rules and argued that the adult's treatment of others ought to be a compound of sympathy and imagination. Rules are for the tyro, and this holds as much for morality as elsewhere. Nowhere is this more obvious than when we come to deal with sexual partnerships. To see that your husband is feeling miserable and insecure requires a sort of insight which depends, not on applying a rule 'When he is miserable, comfort him', but rather on perception. You have first to *see* that this is insecurity, and that requires a sort of sympathetic imagination which may, sometimes though not always, involve putting yourself in his shoes. It is moral perception which is required, and ideally this moral perception develops as two people live together. What it is not is a matter which outside experts can decide on, arriving from the Church marriage advice department equipped with moral slide-rules and a list of maxims.

Because people vary, good marriages vary. One obvious way is in the role sexuality plays. Although another couple's marriage is not only obscure to the outsider but, frequently, even more obscure to the partners (after all, they live it rather than analyse it), I do not doubt that there are good marriages, marked by love, trust and understanding, in which sex plays a small role, just as there are good marriages in which it is essential and central.

The idea of marriage I shall understand promiscuously, as philosophers are wont to say nowadays (though the metaphor is risky here). What I shall say is intended to apply to all relationships in which sexuality is significant, whether the couple are married or no, whether or not they are expected to be permanent, and whether they are homosexual. I preclude only casual relationships.

There is not much to be said for pulling one's punches here, and so I propose to put my position in as combative a way as I can in order to confront Christians with what I see as the failure of the churches to understand marital relationships. I argue that the misunderstandings inherent in conventional Christian views about marriage are so profound as to produce a doctrine that is evil. Does this mean that to hold them or to advocate them is wicked? That, I think, depends. Consider an analogous case, that of racist doctrines. A stupid man or a man who was so under the thumb of a dominant political party that he could not allow that blacks should have equal access to health, education and the redress of the law would not be wicked but merely misguided. A stupid man or a man who was so terrified of defying the church that he could not consider any alternative to its teaching would also not be wicked, merely misguided. We can, as well, easily imagine that somebody might believe the church's teaching on marriage but not put it into practice. Since I take the view that we have a moral obligation to use contraception when it is available and appropriate, I assume that somebody who believes in the papal teaching on contraception but actually uses contraception would be holding evil ideas but acting well, all things being equal, though perversely acting inconsistently or out of weakness of will. Still, as against this, to believe in evil ideas is always a bad thing; consider, too, that you may always be prone to advocate them and that can have a bad effect on others. No doubt, too, you will suffer from unnecessary guilt. Then again there may be simple souls who do not realize the implications of what they are doing, and for them acting on Christian doctrine will not be wrong, for they are not acting badly so much as acting foolishly. But for an intelligent Roman Catholic the situation must be different. For of such people we could say that they could see what is wrong with their actions if they were prepared to think it over.

So far I have said nothing about marriage with which many Christians will not agree. They will agree, too, that both the Anglican marriage service and the Roman Catholic official teaching on the subject show a seriously flawed understanding of what a loving relationship can be. So the badness of the moral teaching derives from a failure to understand the nature of very many good relationships between couples. Many Christians will also agree with me in rejecting the first reason for marriage given in the Book of Common Prayer. This follows St Paul in describing marriage as a necessary provision for the incontinent; it is as though its only justification is that, outside marriage, the man or woman would be licentious and promiscuous. This wretched view of the place of sexual love has had, as many would acknowledge, a disastrous effect on Christian thinking through the ages and its evil effects are evident today, especially in the attitudes of some converts to Roman Catholicism. I shall not discuss this view in any detail. There are no persuasive arguments in its favour and it has few supporters.

The second approach, which I shall describe as 'functionalist', which regards sexual intercourse as primarily a means to the procreation of children with the side-effects that it can strengthen the bond between man and woman, has a little more to recommend it, but only a little (it is again to be found in the Book of Common Prayer). However, entwined with the idea that various part of the body have certain functions specified by God, it leads to the conclusion that intercourse is only permissible when procreation is intended. It is this, of course, which is connected with the idea that contraception is a moral evil.

A more appetizing view of sex is what I shall call the expressionist view which the more attractive Christian thinkers, those not in the grip of a life-denying puritanism, advocate. (*The New Catholic Encyclopaedia* is eloquent on its behalf.) This view takes sexual intercourse to be an expression of love between two people; its intimacy makes it especially important in this respect. Now in reply to this, I do not, of course, deny that sexual intercourse can be expressive, but it is obvious that it is only one of many ways of expressing love, from giving flowers, making phone calls or writing notes to the act of marrying itself. The act of expression is thus externally related to that which it expresses. Other forms of expression are available, and the choice of a means of expression does not change the relationship.

Implicit in my criticisms is, of course, a conception of a loving relationship which recognizes its potentiality. Essential to this is the idea that there are good relationships in which the sexual bond is internal to the nature of the bond. That means that whereas it is conceivable, if the relationship is expressive, that other forms of expression are valid, and that the form of expression chosen does not affect the relationship, for many people, probably the majority, the absence of sexual intercourse changes the relationship and that for the worse.

Now I am inclined to think all other relationships to be different from marriage as far as this is concerned. If a child loves her mother deeply and is in the habit of bringing flowers when visiting, then a failure to do so can be disturbing. But if the child brings something else or explains that she has not had time to buy flowers then it would be, we will agree, irrational for the mother to be hurt and worse for her to be resentful.

But a failure to make love when one's partner wants and needs it is more significant. For resentment is a natural and justifiable reaction from your partner, and that points to the central place of sex in such a relationship. Unless there are reasons, temporary or not, such as infection or menstruation or other matters of health, as to why intercourse should not occur, then resentment is difficult to avoid. If one partner knows that love-making is essential to the security, the confidence in being loved and the general feeling of well-being of the other, then to refuse it is cruel. It is, of course, sometimes a means of manipulation and is the worse on that account. I can imagine a defender of the papal view saying that sex should be avoided where procreation is not intended. But if it is wrong for a partner to take offence it is also wrong to place him or her in a position where he or she is likely to do wrong. Even if you are inclined to take the papal view seriously, which I am not, there is a case for breaking a rule rather than keeping it and causing another to sin.

In Berlioz's wonderful opera *Les Troyens*, Dido learns that, in obedience to the dictate of the Gods, her lover Aeneas is to leave her to go to Italy. In a paroxysm of rage, she turns on him with the unforgettable words

Sexual Love

Monstre de piété! Va donc, va!,
je maudis et tes dieux et toi-même!

That curse, I think, is the entirely proper response of the lover who is expecting and looking forward to a night of passion only to be told that, on the instructions of the church, there is nothing doing.

There is, indeed, an argument relevant here which is probably stronger than any other which I can put forward. What reasons could anybody have for believing in the doctrine of natural law or the church view on marriage or contraception which are so strong as to outweigh that basic moral judgment that it is quite wrong to eschew contraception and not make love to your partner when you both need to. If I were a Christian I would regard contraception, like antibiotics, as one of the great blessings science and technology has brought to humankind.

As I have said, I do not deny that there are many loving relationships in which sexuality is incidental or even perhaps irrelevant. As one gets older, one becomes aware not only of the enormous variety of relationships to which I have already alluded but also of the variety of the ways in which people seem to flourish; one also becomes aware, of course, of the strains which relationships create. That the churches have failed to see this variety is evident from the prevailing view of homosexual relationships. My only claim is that many very good relationships are as I describe and that they have given to our culture paradigms, perhaps unexpressed and unanalysed, but models nonetheless, of what a loving relationship should be. Sometimes, of course, these models are themselves ladders which, once ascended, need to be thrown away. The difficulty is often that a relationship cannot be changed without disruption. As Milan Kundera remarks somewhere, beginning a relationship is like signing a contract. Certain expectations are created in those first few words and the expectations become binding. Nor do I wish to deny that some people may flourish as celibate, necessarily outside the monogamous relationships I am mainly concerned with. However, I imagine that such people will be exceptions and I certainly would vehemently reject any suggestion that celibacy is superior.

The difference between the relation that is intrinsic and the relation that simply has causal consequences for other aspects of the bond is not one of kind but one of degree. What I claim is that the repercussions of sexual abstinence are not single nor limited but pattern themselves over the relationship in such far-reaching and intimate ways that the relationship is changed. It would be strange, if not unthinkable, that the relationship should change if you decide to give your lover chrysanthemums rather than a rose for a birthday. But if it does change, say because a rose has been the traditional birthday present, then the omission signals a change which has already begun to take place. The gift expresses that change. But we all expect a relationship itself to change if the couple stop making love. For sexual intercourse is not an optional way of expressing love. One reason is that it is the *telos* of an activity of caressing and, as a general rule, neither party will be completely satisfied with anything short of it. In this respect it is as much part of our nature as the need to eat and drink. Our bodies demand it. Mutual desirability is normally part of the groundwork of a decent relationship. The awareness that the other partner can, if he or she chooses, desist is liable to be devastating.

Sexual Love

The immediate consequence of the fact that sexual intercourse is intrinsic to the bond, when added to the evident fact that not only can the earth not support a large increase in population but neither can the loving bond between two people usually negotiate a large family, is that to avoid the use of contraception is morally wrong and to advocate that people should eschew it is wicked. But the wrongness of the attitude of some Christians to contraception derives from the consequences that doctrine has. What is intrinsically evil is the conception of love which produces such consequences. If human beings were very much less fertile than they are and the average family size, despite the most strenuous attempts, never edged above replacement, then there might be no need for contraception and it would be pointless trying to ban it. Such a scenario is more than a possibility if males continue to become less fertile (which might be just about the best piece of news we have had of late). But, in such circumstances, where a couple was having sexual intercourse hundreds of times a year without producing children, nevertheless, it could be still mistakenly viewed as functional or expressive and it would represent a serious moral error to see it in that light.

The intrinsic nature of the relationship between a bond and sexual intercourse is perhaps best understood with reference to some ideas which are familiar in another area of philosophy, aesthetics. Think about cutting a play or an opera or altering the dimensions of a painting in order to hang it in one particular spot in your room. If you alter or delete a passage in a poem or part of a painting, your vandalism generally has implications, and the finer the piece the larger the consequences. A cut, say, in a mature quartet by Mozart will mean that the interrelationships and the balance of the parts is no longer the same. A major alteration may mean that it will cease to have the character it had before. In the same way a loving relationship which was sexual and ceases to be so is very likely to change radically and most often for the worse. So if a couple have regularly had intercourse in an attempt to have a family and then, when the family is complete, they cease, we cannot expect the relationship to stay the same. If it does, it suggests that the sexuality was not central. Perhaps, where there was, for example, intense jealousy, abstinence might represent an improvement. But such cases will be exceptional.

Sexual frustration can have moral consequences. First, as I have remarked before, people in a loving relationship tend to be happier, and happier people are better people, almost without exception. The Chinese writer, Jung Chang, remarks, 'When people are happy, they are kind.' Many writers have described how, with the loss of regular sexual intercourse, a couple loses that intimacy, that undemanding and unstressful concern for each other which is so important to the partners. A strangeness and distance creeps in. A relationship which was once central to their lives becomes peripheral. Perhaps it is not surprising that the celibates who originally promulgated church teaching should not have the imagination to appreciate this. It is perhaps not easy for them to see either that marriage is a vale of soul-making. A deep relationship requires one taking responsibility for another; his or her well-being comes to matter more to you than your own and, unlike a parent-child relationship, this relationship is reciprocal. But like having a child, taking a partner is giving a hostage to fortune; you have placed your well-being at the mercy of chance. Many of us would say that without a partner or a child we remain shallow. This is not true of everybody, of course, but it is true of many. Often a spinster or a bachelor will seem to the parent or to the married not to have grown up. Of course, there is also another side to this. Married couples sometimes seem to build a wall around themselves. Their relationship is so dense and compact that it finds little room for others. What they do for others has become, in a sense, external to them.

6

Immortality

Christians believe that death, were there nothing after it, must be an evil. The hope of a life to come is central to their faith and it is that prospect which makes the death that ends an earthly life not an evil but a gateway to something better. So their conception of a good life is not one which comes to an end with death. If life was like this, then, although there would be good things about some lives such as love, pleasure and the appreciation of beauty, in general our lives would be diminished by their finitude. Now if an endless life is a good for man, then we should find it a desirable prospect, given a clear sighting of it. In the words of Isaac Watts,

> Could we but climb where Moses stood,
> And view the landscape o'er;
> Not Jordan's stream nor death's cold flood,
> Should fright us from the shore.

I do not find the idea of a life after death attractive and I cannot imagine that an endless life would be a good life to lead.

But before I discuss this, we ought first of all to think about death. I said that Christians commonly think of death as something evil and that it is only the prospect of an after-life which makes it not so. But should we think of death as an evil at all? Philosophers from Epicurus onwards have discussed this. I do not intend to pursue their arguments here; rather, I want to approach this question from a slightly different angle from that taken by many previous thinkers.

To ask whether death is an evil or not, without specifying a context, is to ask a question which has no answer. When any individual dies it makes good sense to ask whether or not her death is an evil, and the answer to that question is pretty obvious. Sometimes it is and sometimes it isn't. If she is old, tired, ill, facing increasing pain and aware of fading mental powers, she may welcome death, and for her, death may be a good thing. For a young man whose life is thrown away in a futile war engineered by a political leader who thinks it is in her interests or the interests of her party to fight a war on this particular issue, death is a largely unmitigated evil. Context is everything and the question as to whether death is an evil aside from a specific context is a completely futile question. Of course if the old lady's position were different, her death might be an evil, and if the young man's position were different; if, for example, he had, unbe-knownst to himself, contracted a virulent form of a painful disease, his death might not be such an unmitigated evil. There is no sense in claiming that death is intrinsically an evil, by which we presumably mean that, aside from a context, death is always bad. For there is no such thing as death without a context. Death is the end of somebody's life, and that life must have a character of some sort or another.

What may be true is that, as the philosopher Bernard Williams remarks, the majority of deaths are either too early or too late, and in that sense the majority of deaths are not goods for the individual or her family. But a death might be timed to perfection, though it is unlikely we could be sure that that is so, since we could never be sure that the individual might not have a few more weeks or months of lucidity and worthwhile life.

However, the question I have raised is whether a life that does not terminate with death but rather goes on endlessly is a good life to lead. Once again let me stress that I am not concerned with the question whether in fact I shall wake up in some different state after my death. I suppose it is evident that I do not believe this for a minute, partly because it does not seem to me to be a very coherent idea. Rather, I am concerned as to whether it is sensible to desire this and whether it would be welcome if it occurred. (After all, that something is impossible does not prevent us from wanting it; we can have incoherent desires; I might wish to discover a perpetual motion machine.) Nor shall I discuss the possibility that the next life might be no improvement on the present. In fact there seems no special reason to suppose that it is, even for the righteous. If God made this world, why should the next be any better? Of course, religious leaders tell us it is better. But they do not know and there is no good reason to believe them.

One of the best known essays by Bernard Williams is called 'The Makropulos Case: Reflections on the Tedium of Immortality'. The title refers to an opera by the great Czech composer Leos Janacek which is, in turn, based on a play by Karel Capek. The plot is this. A sixteenth-century court physician Hieronymus Makropulos discovers the elixir of human life. His emperor, Rudolph II of Hapsburg, insists that he first try it out on his sixteen-year-old daughter,

Elena. She lives for 300 years under various changes of name. By the time the action of the opera starts, her life has sunk into *ennui;* she is sated with it; her only fleeting interest is her own past and her only motivation is her fear of death. The climax of the opera, as Elena ages before our eyes, is her acceptance of death at last and her realization how much she wants to die. The recipe for the elixir is thrown into the fire. Life requires death. Without death life would not be more to be enjoyed but less.

Now Elena lives for over three hundred years. But Christians hold out before us the prospect of immortality. The Shorter Catechism says that the chief end of man is to glorify God and to enjoy him for ever. Let me postpone the idea of 'enjoying God' for the moment and concentrate instead, more generally, on the idea of 'enjoyment' *simpliciter*. What sorts of things do we enjoy? The activities we choose to engage in during our spare time range widely. I read a book which I find absorbing, swim or cycle if the weather is fine, lie on the beach in the sun, play the piano, do crosswords, watch films, go to the theatre, go to a concert, listen to records, argue and read the newspapers. Most of these things require no great effort of concentration; some do. In reading a really good book I am carried along. That is not to say my intelligence is not active. It is, but it is no effort to apply it. Doing a crossword may be interesting. Even though it requires no effort to concentrate upon it, it is difficult, difficult enough to exercise me. I succeed against obstacles.

I said that applying my mind to an interesting book may be no hardship but it does require intellectual effort. There is, too, a distinction between making myself read a book which is difficult and dull (a daily exercise which occupied me for a large part of my life as an academic) and picking up something which is difficult but interesting.

There are of course many exceptions to the rule that what we enjoy involves working against obstacles. Some of those I listed do not require working against obstacles. There are, for example, the pleasures of eating, drinking and making love though, for some people, obstacles arbitrarily set up turn the last into a form of sport. And since some wines are described as 'easy drinking', some other wines must be difficult drinking, I suppose. Games, though, usually involve the setting up of arbitrary obstacles. Try to hit three upright sticks at a distance of twenty-two yards with a ball of specified weight and diameter without bending the arm at the elbow whilst somebody else defends them with a piece of wood. Even when you can regularly pitch the ball on a length, part of the pleasure lies in the practice required to achieve this; the pleasure depends on the difficulty with which that skill has been obtained. There would be no pleasure in getting a hole-in-one at golf if I could do it at will. As Goethe remarked, 'I should not know what to do with eternal bliss if it did not present me with new problems and difficulties to overcome.'

So what about enjoying God? What sort of enjoyment could I have of God's presence? Do I contemplate him as a natural wonder, a sort of divine Niagara Falls? The pleasures of natural phenomena seem likely to be less rewarding than the pleasures I sketched in the previous section. I can weary of looking at a good view particularly if, unlike my local landscape, it does not change with the light, the weather and the seasons. (And God is immutable.) Is it not plausible to suppose that I would weary of contemplating God? Unless God is as most Christians imagine him, somebody like a vain, cruel, intolerant, political ruler, he would not be at all put out if I said, 'Right, I've had a good look for a few months – now has St Peter got the *Independent* crossword?' or, 'Is that J.S.Bach I see over there, do you think he could spare a few months to teach me how to write a decent mirror fugue?' It may, of course, be that the appreciation of God requires effort and preparation on our part measured by years of soul-making in this life. It may even be that we arrive in heaven with different capacities to understand, capacities which a heavenly existence does nothing to enlarge. Some of us, such as those who die in infancy, even if baptized before their death, will live on in a semi-cretinous existence. Perhaps St Anthony, that unfortunate saint who is regularly thanked through the Roman Catholic press for helping people to find lost articles (the hammer which was put down heaven knows where, the lost kitten, the photograph of Aunt Mabel or the key of the Black and Decker), is a saint of unusual dimness (though apparently he reads the papers). He has been assigned to more lowly duties, whilst St Thomas Aquinas spends his hours in intellectual contemplation. On the other hand, it may be that in heaven we develop intellectual capacities which we do not now have such that we can consider the complexities of pure Being along with St Thomas.

Even supposing that there are conditions like this under which the heavenly life would not be the ultimate in boredom, we are still left with the fact that it goes on for ever. Human beings, we can safely declare, get tired of anything in time. We require the stimulus of new ideas, new interests and some changes (and if God is infinite in His variety we have to face the unpalatable fact that he is also immutable). To adore God for ever requires that he reveals different sides of his character to us from time to time. 'So, you are bored with my justice; why not contemplate my love for a century or two?' But even if we return to the contemplation of God at intervals, it still lasts an eternity and Bernard Williams' objection is still terminal. More thought should have been put to the writing of the Shorter Catechism.

I can imagine a believer now saying, 'You consider God from a human perspective. However, not only do we not grasp his nature but we do not grasp what it would be like so to change as to enjoy his nature in heaven.'

This leads us to new and interesting problems. Set aside the fact that, as usual, we are asked to sign a blank cheque in these respects. We are given no reasons for assuming that, in heaven, we might not change so that we lose whatever limited capacity we have to enjoy God, or that, having changed, we find that coming to understand God makes his nature more alien and terrifying still. Religious believers are shameless in committing themselves to speculations which present us with what they think to be an enticing picture of the afterlife that they and their co-believers will enjoy. But we have no reason at all to suppose that that is how it will be. Nevertheless, in some respects, this is the least of our problems. What we are being told here is that it makes sense to want a state which we would have to have different desires in order to enjoy. Can I have a desire which is conditional on very extensive changes in myself for its satisfaction?

Consider some more down-to-earth cases. Painting is not a very important part of my life. I rarely go into art galleries, though good architecture and townscapes do give me a great deal of pleasure; my eye is not entirely untrained. I can imagine what it must be like to enjoy painting much more fully than I do because I have, on a few occasions, been transfixed by a painting in the way I am often moved by music. A painting can occasionally move me to tears. I can see, as well, that I would take more pleasure in my surroundings if my eye was trained by familiarity with a tradition of painting and drawing. But, for some reason, I do not seek it out in the way I do film, music and literature. Perhaps my life does not contain the space for another passion of that sort. In a parallel way I have friends who are moved by music, but would not bother to go to concerts regularly and do not persevere with music. Their attitude to music is much like mine to painting. Part of music being an interest for me is that I am prepared to put up with hearing a good deal of mediocre music which I do not like or which I find boring. But mixed in with this are those pieces which I love deeply and which I need to hear regularly. I rarely have a sudden passion to see a painting which I like in the way I have a sudden passion to hear some music or to play a piece or to read a poem.

Because painting is not a passion, the sense in which I can think of myself as 'missing it' is etiolated. I register the fact that my life is the poorer for not enjoying painting. But I do not 'miss' it in the sense of having a sense of loss, the sense of loss I may have if somebody has borrowed a favourite CD and I suddenly want to hear it. Do I wish that I did love the visual arts? If I do, the wish is paper-thin. It is a thought, a possibility, but I do not suffer. It is not a powerful desire. Like many of our wishes, it is perfunctory. People sometimes say to me, 'How I wish I enjoyed music as you do', or, 'How I wish I could play the piano'. In most cases the wish is idle. Other people had piano lessons as children but did not care for it enough to enjoy practising and playing. If they could play now, it is questionable whether they would play. Either it is a controlling passion or it is not and if it is not, then the loss expressed in 'How I wish. . .' is sentimental or self-deceiving.

Transfer this to the case of a longing for a heavenly life and much the same applies. I cannot really desire it very strongly. Schweitzer talks about the 'heavenly home-sickness' in Bach's great and much-loved cantata *'Ich habe genug'* (BWV 82). The German title is sensibly translated 'It is enough' and it expresses a profound weariness. No doubt the desire for heaven was the desire for rest and was perfectly intelligible for the vast majority of people in earlier centuries who were overworked, underfed and trodden down by the rich. But I doubt whether the rich felt that way. Nowadays in the West there is sufficient leisure for many people to imagine that a heavenly life as outlined in hymns is extremely boring. Rest is not what they crave. John Stuart Mill put it well. 'In a happier condition of human life, not annihilation but immortality may be the burdensome idea.'

So what of desires which are not those which I rarely have, like my desire to appreciate painting more than I do, but which I have never had? Some of these will be desires which, in a good sense of 'imagine', I cannot even imagine having. I cannot imagine how a man can get an orgasm through arson so, for me, the sexual pleasure involved in fire-lighting is in that sense unimaginable. These are objects of passion which I cannot desire, even feebly, and I certainly do not miss them. How can I imagine having the desire to sing God's praises around his throne, even for an hour or two? I can certainly imagine enjoying a good sing-song, but that does not seem to be the point at issue. I do not feel any desire to sing his praises, nor do I feel any loss at not having the chance to do so, and I very strongly suspect that those who think they do confuse the genuine pleasure of community singing with the pleasure of praising God. Still, I may be wrong about this, and it certainly does not matter to the argument. My concern is that I cannot now have a desire conditional on a change of state in me in such a way that that desire will now materialize, and so I cannot have a sense of loss at the absence of that object or state which, were I different, I would desire. My wife has no sense of loss in lacking the (dubious) pleasure of supporting one side in a competitive team sport because such sports do not interest her. So a heavenly life in which I spend eternity praising God is not, as far as I am concerned, a desirable prospect.

Now a counter-argument immediately presents itself. It is possible to envisage changes in myself so that what is not now desirable becomes desirable. To a healthy woman in the prime of life the thought of death might seem terrible but, obviously, if you are very old and feeble or in extreme pain, the prospect of death may be a prospect of release. In a different state, there are different desires. It is hard for somebody in the middle of life to focus on desires which are conditional on changes in her such that she no longer has much in the way of desires, interests or plans or they no longer matter to her. We ought not to confuse the fear of imminent death (which may be reasonable) with the fear of eventual death (which is not). Our problems in facing death certainly involve a failure to keep these apart. I certainly cannot have the desire for death given my present good health, plans and enjoyment of life. But I can see that there may come a point when death seems to me desirable. Equally, I will agree that people may desire a heavenly life in a weak sense of desire. They have been told that it offers experiences beyond compare and on that testimony regard it as desirable.

So I do not maintain that people do not, in fact, desire heaven. I think they do. What I do think is that in very many cases the desires are not coherent. It is certainly possible for me to desire something which cannot be made plausibly desirable under any descriptions I give of it. It is also true that a believer might say she desires to be in heaven, believe that she wants to be in heaven and yet not really want to be in heaven; we see this if she declines the offer of martyrdom. A friend of mine who never went anywhere except to visit his mother on the other side of the country declared that his ambition was to travel. But since he never made any attempt to do so, it was obviously false.

I have said that the accounts given of the heavenly life do not make it desirable to me now. It would only become desirable to me if considerable changes took place in me. But then there is a question as to whether the changed state could itself seem desirable to me now. This surely is crucial. What is required is that I desire to be in the state where I form new desires, desires which I do not have until I am in that state. Some such changes have been and do seem to be desirable to the person concerned. A drug addict might wish his state to change to a state where he no longer desired drugs. Certainly I might wish that I liked expensive wine less; somebody might wish that she did not have certain sexual desires which are difficult or painful to fulfil. At the extreme, some religious people have wished for a state where all desire ceases; I assume they really wanted it, though it seems to me quite as undesirable as anything else I have considered. For to want to be in a state where I have no desires, plans or wishes at all seems to me no better than death. In any case, even in a situation where I want to change my state and in changing that state acquire different desires, there needs to be some continuity in my personality. Some changes are such that I would not be able to recognize myself as being the same person. Changing into an Azande or an Amazonian Indian with all the ideas and beliefs which go with their existence is a change which I cannot conceive of as a change in *me*. It is rather the replacement of me by somebody else. No more have I a desire to enter a state in which I would be satisfied by praising God for eternity. To be in such a state, as it seems to me now, would be to have lost whatever powers of taste and discrimination I now have. The crucial point is that to make sense of the present desirability of an eternal life, what I do in that life has to be related to what I desire and what I do in this.

The best analogies for the way Christians think about heaven are earthly. A pubescent child might want a sexual outlet of which she is unconscious because she cannot imagine it. It does not follow that she does not want it because she does not consciously want it. In such a case 'want' is close to 'need'. In parallel a believer can now argue that I need a heavenly life even if I neither want it nor know I need it, but that, since God knows I need it, he supplies it. But if this is not to be quite a pallid sense of 'want' as opposed to 'need', a mere intellectual recognition, it depends on the assumption that without God I am uneasy and uncomfortable and frustrated. I am a bit like the sexually frustrated teenager. I might be aware of missing something and not know what it is. The idea is expressed beautifully in the words of St Augustine, 'Our hearts are restless till they find their rest in thee.'

But suppose I feel no such thing. I feel no discomfort in my present state. Nobody has managed to 'convict me of sin'. Then the sentiment of wanting a heavenly life comes to little more than assent to a proposition. It is not different in principle from wanting to enjoy painting because I see my friends enjoying it but without having a strong desire for it.

The natural response of the believer to this argument will be that I do not have such a desire because I lack the spirituality which other, more fortunate, people have. My belief that the religious view of the good life is not a good life for me is just plain wrong. I would flourish in such a heavenly life and I ought to be discontented with this life and long for the next. Such an existence is more authentic, more attuned to underlying realities than the life I now lead. That I do not recognize this merely points up a failing in me.

My reply to this is to recall Bernard Williams's observation that eternal life must necessarily be tedious. Such a life cannot be desirable simply because it is endless. In such an existence, there is no reason to do one thing rather than another at any one time because eternity lies before us. It is a recipe for an utterly destructive *ennui* and indolence. There are a few concluding reflections which may reinforce this.

There is such a thing as being bored with oneself, with one's limited interests, capacities and horizons. This is not the same as being bored with the things which used to amuse you. You can become bored with those, of course. But there is a certain sort of self-recognition where you see that the fault lies in yourself. You are too ingrained in your interests and concerns for it to be possible to form new ones. And yet you are tired of the old ones. Of course, most people who are bored are bored because they lack the resources to form interests and enthusiasms. They are the people of rather limited capacities who 'have to be amused'. I am not speaking of them. I am speaking of people who have long-term interests, tire of them and yet cannot change them. I have sometimes wished that philosophy was not such an addiction for me. I want a change not so much from philosophy as from being the sort of person I am. This preoccupation may be one of the 'gifts reserved for age', as T.S. Eliot ironically put it; it may, of course, connect with declining powers which make the pursuit of these interests frustrating. Intellectuals certainly suffer from this. But if I can feel like that late in this life, boredom with myself surely becomes almost inevitable in eternity. To suppose that I could change and take on new interests, become, for example, passionately interested in breeding hamsters (which is something which would have to be as abstract a discipline as pure mathematics in a world where nothing dies and nothing is born), is to suppose that I would change in ways which at present I cannot countenance and certainly do not want. For I do not desire to breed hamsters now and I do not desire to be in a state in which hamster-breeding becomes my passion. There is no connection between that eternal life and this such that I can find it now desirable.

Apart from your motivations, you might also be bored with your regrets, remembered embarrassments and resentments. Life has become tedious because you are imprisoned within the sort of person you are. I have said that something like this can happen to the old. It connects with my suspicion that there is an extraordinary and very shallow egotism built into the Christian desire for immortality. For we cannot think away the contingencies of life. It has a natural rise and fall. Our physical and mental faculties wax and wane. Evolution, which brought humankind to the point where it can frame such speculations, would not have occurred without the death of the individual. That is essential for natural selection. The existence of people who can enjoy life, enjoy reflection and fear death is conditional on their dying in turn.

I speak for myself only when I say that I do not think I am interesting enough for a sensible God to keep me in existence for an eternity. He would find me boring and I would be bored with him. Nor can I conceive how I would relate to a community of millions of souls. Already there are too many human beings in this world whose composite creative output is too great for us to comprehend. We are lost in our cultures in a way which was not true even only forty years ago. So how could we other than flounder when dealing with countless millions of souls in aeons of time? And to imagine changes to myself such that I could comprehend what was going on is to imagine changes which make me so unlike my present self that there is no longer a sense of continuity.

I will end on a recollection. I once dreamt that death was not the end of my life but that I awoke to another life which was inexplicable, chaotic and terrifying, much like the initial impact of a world very unlike this. Perhaps, if the newborn baby had some Platonic knowledge of a previous existence which it brought with it, this life would seem equally frightening. My dream reinforced my wonder that people should want a life after death. I can imagine that some would like a better life than they have had on earth. I have been immensely lucky to live in a country which, after my childhood, was at peace, prosperous by historical standards and not marked by the oppression of the poor by the rich to anything like the extent normal in human history.

Immortality

For people during most of the Christian era the option of another life in which they had a better fist of opportunities than this was extremely attractive. The text from *Des Knaben Wunderhorn* set by Mahler as the finale of his Fourth Symphony expresses the idea of a future life marked by a plentiful supply of bread, meat and fish, music and dancing.

Gut' Kräuter von allerhand Arten,
Die wachsen in himmlischen Garten!
Gut' Spargel, Fisolen,
Und was wir nur wollen!
Ganz Schüsseln voll sind uns bereit!

Good greens of all sorts
grow in the garden of heaven,
good asparagus, runner beans,
and whatever we wish for,
whole dishes are ready for us.

Such naiveties aside, the prospect of life after death does not attract. Mankind's fear of the uncanny surely gives us grounds enough to fear another life.

7

Epilogue

'Faith is a sore affliction; like loving somebody who
is out there in the dark; silent, unresponsive'
(from Ingmar Bergmann, *The Seventh Seal*)

I

Nobody now supposes that the arguments once thought to
show the existence of God actually work. Whereas people
once thought that the presence of cause and effect in the
universe required that the causal chain originated with God as
the first cause or that the universe exhibits design and design
requires a Designer, Hume's classical discussion in his
Dialogues on Natural Religion destroyed these arguments.
What lingering attachment we might have to the argument
from design was disposed of by Darwinian theory. What
appearance there is of design is accounted for by evolution
working through natural selection. Once God's existence was
part of common sense. But the place for religion in our lives
and society has largely vanished, and the clock cannot be
turned back. It is not that people do not believe and worship;
they do, but religion has lost its confidence and its central place
in our lives, and believers are on the defensive.

Epilogue

Even atheists might regret this, partly because we have detached ourselves from the roots of our culture. Our art, music and literature are deeply imbued with Christianity. The place of the Bible in moulding English prose can hardly be overestimated. I belong to the last generation in whom a knowledge of the Bible and prayer book can simply be assumed. My younger friends and colleagues have lost an essential part of English culture, and a central reference point has disappeared.

Still, regrettable or not, the intellectual climate has changed, and religion occupies a small corner of it. Given what I have said, it will be assumed by most of my readers that I think religious belief is irrational and regrettable, and it will also be assumed that I think religion is in conflict with science and that science gives the answers, or a promise of the answers which religion has failed to provide. If we want the truth about the world and if we want intellectually satisfying explanations, science will do the job. In fact I subscribe to neither of these beliefs.

Firstly, I do not think that religious belief is necessarily irrational. The immediate reaction of a reader who is thinking along with me might be to assume that I have in mind primitive or uneducated people, say in rural Poland or Ireland, where the church has a stranglehold upon their minds. In such a situation a belief in animism or in the miracle-working powers of an image of the Virgin Mary will not be irrational. No more was the belief of the ancient Jews, ignorant of the nature of animal digestion, that a time would come when the lion will lie down with the lamb.

Yes, I do agree that these are some of the people whose religious beliefs we cannot call irrational. Western science has had no impact upon their societies and there is no

93

critical tradition. But whilst it is not irrational for one of the Nyoro to believe that his child is ill because the ghost of his father is angry, equally it does not seem to me irrational for a modern Western Christian to maintain his religious beliefs in the face of objections. He finds some way in which he can continue to believe in the Real Presence despite its defiance of common sense. I find it unsurprising and in a way honourable that people brought up in a church continue to stay with it. It is their church and their community, and to leave it is disloyal. It is their family. Losing your faith is profoundly disturbing. It is like falling out of love; bit by bit your attitude to the loved one changes; you see flaws you did not see before; what once seemed endearing now irritates; what was central to your life becomes peripheral, until one day you realize, perhaps with relief, perhaps with horror, perhaps quite suddenly, that you no longer love him. But it is reasonable to fight this process. We cannot convict those who choose to stay and fight off objections of irrationality just like that. It depends just how many of the old beliefs have been sloughed off, just how much of the ritual and the characteristic modes of speech are now alien and rebarbative.

But it is one thing to stay with a church despite progressive disagreements on doctrine, and quite another to join a church in the face of such obstacles. Converts to the church do what those brought up in it do not have to do; they sign on the dotted line. So for an outsider a spectacle like the recent Gadarene rush of Anglicans to join the Roman Catholic Church because they object to women priests is both puzzling and alarming. The decision to 'go over' is rational and understandable if the man (and it is nearly always a man) has been teetering on the brink for a long time and the ordination of women is the last straw. But it is hardly likely to be true of all of these and surely not true of all the members of the congregations. If you are 'received', as the jargon goes, you accept 'all that the church teaches', including notorious stumbling blocks such as papal infallibility. How come that these people can accept what they could not accept before? It strains credulity that the grounds for these bizarre beliefs become apparent to thousands of people simultaneously. It strains credulity even more to suppose that an objection to women priests suddenly produces a belief in a number of rather silly dogmas. The desire for the illusory security of a dogmatic church overwhelms what critical faculties they have. This is irrationality with a vengeance, and either dishonesty or self-deception must play a large part. But whereas for an educated Westerner to convert, whether to Catholic, Evangelical or Buddhist varieties, must always carry the suspicion of treachery as well as irrationality, to remain with the beliefs with which you were imbued as a child does not seem to me irrational.

Of course, I would not say this if I believed that the standard of rationality is given by natural science. For much of the past two centuries there has been an assumption that the methods of the natural sciences define what it is to be rational. Science involves the discipline of checking one's beliefs against independent facts, and this has been one of the great virtues of Western thought. Religion fails to do this and can therefore be dismissed as irrational. Furthermore, natural science progressively approximates to an accurate picture of the world, and in such a picture there is, as Laplace famously observed, no need for the hypothesis of a God. Now I, too, would deny that there are other substances such as God or mind-stuff to which we need to refer in explaining what goes on in the world. There is just the physical world. But to admit this is not to concede that all 'real' explanations are physical in nature. We cannot 'in principle', as they say, reduce psychology or even biology to bio-chemistry and bio-chemistry to physics, as the 'unified science movement' of the 1930s claimed. To say this is not to claim advance knowledge of what physics will or will not achieve in the future. To make such predictions would be foolish. What shows the limitations of physics is the matter of what can count as an explanation. Even if I could explain the sounds I make when speaking to my friends in terms of brain events connecting the two according to physical laws, that would not explain why I was rude to somebody. Nor can we expect, in the fullness of time, to explain in terms of physical laws and initial conditions why Mozart wrote an apparently trivial ending to *Don Giovanni*. This has nothing to do with the fact that the initial conditions are not to hand. Even if they were, and even if we could then produce an immaculate concatenation of causes and effects leading up to Mozart's inscription on the manuscript paper, it simply would not explain what we want to explain.

There is, of course, a perfectly good sense in which physics is fundamental. We would not have had a Mozart if we did not have a material world which, as it happens, has carbon-based life forms. But the universe has changed. What once could be explained satisfactorily in terms of physical laws alone, such as changes on the earth's crust or even simple forms of life such as the amoeba or earthworms where any responses are merely physico-chemical reactions to stimuli, gave way to more complex forms of life, and to explain these we need, first of all, concepts like aim and purpose and, latterly, concepts like belief. These explanations are progressively difficult to replace by simpler cause-effect relationships bound together by laws of nature. Eventually the connection becomes so tortuous that the sense of an explanation altogether vanishes. Just as I cannot explain my typing the words I type on my word processor by reference to my learning English as a toddler, no more can I explain my intentions by reference to what currently happens in my brain. There was a time, millions and millions of years ago, when, had there been anybody around to explain what was happening on the earth, the explanation would have been in purely physical terms. (Though, of course, the very assumption of an explainer rules out a purely physical picture of understanding.)

II

As I have said, theology and morality are not independent. Our morality dictates how we characterize God. But the influence is one-way. It does not follow from the dependence of theology on morality that morality cannot be free from theological suppositions. Obviously I think it can be. I believe in the autonomy of morality in that sense. God is not required to guarantee morality; all the sureties and recognizances of morality are internal. My claim has been that providing a theological framework despoils morality. Some virtues cease to be virtues when given a religious context. Consequently a religious life is not, in many respects, a good life to lead. The religious vision of the good life does not command our allegiance.

I want to stress, even if it is not already plain, that I have few quarrels with the teaching of Jesus. I do not want to replace Christian values with others in the manner of Nietzsche and I have tried, as far as possible, to develop the argument on the basis of values shared by Christians and non-Christians, though I suppose it must be obvious that the values which I assume are largely the product of Christian teaching. This is so even though many Christians, the members of many American sects, many Evangelicals and some Roman Catholics, live by values which seem to me as abhorrent as what is sometimes presented as Islamic law. But what is taught by the major churches is rarely morally objectionable, and where it is, as in the case of its sexual morality, it is something which, however deep-rooted, could be reformed and is, I think, in the process of being changed. Admittedly Manichaeism is still a deep feature of Christian ethics and to expunge it will require, as always, a painful readjustment. The church would have to see that celibacy is not a necessary accompaniment to goodness (I avoid the unpleasant connotations of 'holiness' or piety).

But that a better pattern for everyday morality could be discovered than that which can be found in the Beatitudes, I rather doubt. As a basis for how you deal with friends, colleagues and acquaintances, the suggestions that you neither condemn nor judge, that you forgive and that you do good to your enemies are fundamental. In saying this, I do not renege on my claims that patterns of moral behaviour are for the immature. In accepting these rules we still have to apply them, and their application will need imagination and insight. Not only will it need insight to see why somebody did what he did, but it may need insight to see how to do him good. I have to ask what I can say which will not hinder him. The Beatitudes are no substitute for wisdom.

What is also true, and perhaps on reflection not very surprising, is that these values themselves change in the context of the somewhat stoical morality which I have been advocating.

What I have in mind is something like this. A good man neither pursues a vendetta nor, indeed, needs to forgive those who act against him. The reason is that either in the end the injury no longer matters very much and it is petty to bear a grudge, or so much time has passed that reprisals are pointless. Is this perhaps not forgiveness at all? I am not sure. What I am certain of is that any discomfort between you and the person who has injured you must be embarrassment rather than a lingering resentment. In the same way to do good to your enemies may also be motivated by the thought that it would be small-minded to do otherwise.

What is true is that to recognize the pettiness of non-forgiveness is to make forgiveness less of a big deal. It is utterly central to Christian ethics partly because, by taking wrong-doing to be a sin, the evil even of a peccadillo is magnified by the theological content; this comes out in a phrase like 'All our righteousness is as filthy rags'. But in the sort of post-Christian humanist ethics which I advocate, the virtue of forgiveness, if it is forgiveness which I have described, becomes fairly trivial. Perhaps it is not so surprising that, given that taking virtues into a theological context alters them, removing them also transforms them.

I suppose it is obvious that I do not think that religious education or indoctrination is going to do anything to raise the moral tone of society. The threat of hellfire might induce people who believe in hell to avoid actions which they might otherwise contemplate and this, I suspect, is at the back of the minds of those who advocate compulsory religious education. Their concern is public safety rather than morality. There is, of course, every reason why public safety should be a matter of concern, but it ought not to be confused with morality. It is because religion is deeply imbued with morality that we automatically think of religious education as a means of moral improvement. But to avoid crime because you fear ultimate punishment is not the same as avoiding crime because it is wrong. Most criminals find it hard to take the long view anyway, and the question of whether the prospect of divine punishment is believable at the turn of the second millenium is begged.

Notes

Chapter 1

The quotation from Nancy Mitford is from her *Letters*, ed. Charlotte Mosley, Sceptre 1993, 311.
The quotation from P.T. Geach is from his *The Virtues*, Cambridge University Press 1977, 114.

Chapter 2

I have been influenced by R.W.Beardsmore's 'Atheism and Morality', in *Religion and Morality*, ed. D.Z. Phillips, Macmillan and St Martin's Press 1996.

Chapter 4

Lars Hertzberg's 'On the Attitude of Trust', *Inquiry* 1988 and reprinted in *The Limits of Experience*. *Acta Philosophica Fennica* 1994, stimulated much of this chapter.

Chapter 5

A version of this chapter appeared in *Philosophy Now*, 1995.
The quotation from Jung Chang comes from *Wild Swans*, Harper Collins 1992, 466.

Chapter 6

Bernard Williams's essay 'The Makropulos Case. Reflections on the Tedium of Immortality', appeared in his *Problems of the Self,* Cambridge University Press 1973.